D0342609

Praise for *Costovation*

•

"Being 'low cost' and being 'innovative' are two universal aspirations, but there is exceptionally little information about companies that satisfactorily do both. *Costovation* is brimming with guidance on how to apply innovation principles deep within your business, helping you both nail your market and shield against competitors."

—VIJAY GOVINDARAJAN,
Coxe distinguished professor, Dartmouth Tuck School of Business

"*Costovation* is a must-read if you are looking to beat the cost curve and build businesses that deeply resonate with customers without breaking their wallets. It is bursting with new case studies, step-by-step processes, and practical applications."

—JONATHAN BRILL,
global futurist, HP

"I have found *Costovation* to be the first book to bring together affordability and innovation with such a focus and in an easy-to-apply context that can work for companies large and small. Based on their extensive research, the authors reveal patterns behind the glitzy successes and thus show leaders and innovators how to make it happen in their organizations."

—HENNING TRILL,
head of corporate innovation, Bayer

"So much of the potential for big innovation occurs within a company, not just in what the company delivers to its customers. *Costovation* gives helpful guidance on how to find those big opportunities."

—DAN WALKER,
head of emerging and disruptive technology, BP

"Shifting business models is no easy task. Thankfully, Wunker and Law have outlined a process that's full of concrete examples, detailed guides, and practical advice. *Costovation* is both a highly useful tool and a fascinating read."

—NEIL ALLISON,
director of business model innovation, Pearson

"Must innovation and cost-cutting always be at odds? The authors draw upon decades of innovation experience to introduce a class of innovations that cut costs as much as they delight customers. Whether or not you have 'innovation' in your job title, you'll find this book a stand-out tool to help you transform your business."

—ANISH SHAH,
group president of strategy, Mahindra

"The fast-paced world of delivering quality workplace health and wellness services is both rewarding and complex, and we are constantly thinking about how to maintain our disruptive innovation advantage. *Costovation* provides us with the roadmap to do so, helping us to exceed our customers' needs by rethinking price, value, and delivery models. A must-read for each of us who desires to create true, meaningful, and sustainable value."

—CROCKETT DALE,
CEO, Healthstat

cost·o·vation

cost·o·vation

1. / innovation that gives your customers exactly what they want—and nothing more /

2. / Stephen Wunker and Jennifer Law /

HarperCollins
Leadership
An Imprint of HarperCollins

Published by HarperCollins Leadership, an imprint of HarperCollins.

Book design by Elyse Strongin, Neuwirth & Associates.

ISBN 978-0-8144-3976-0 (eBook)

Library of Congress Control Number: 2018940799

ISBN 978-0-8144-3975-3

Printed in the United States of America
18 19 20 21 22 LSC 10 9 8 7 6 5 4 3 2 1

/ contents /

/ part one /

introduction to costovation

chapter 1

•

What Costovation Is and
Why It Matters

Aside from its electrifying bright purple and yellow decor, Planet Fitness looks like any other gym: There are rows and rows of elliptical machines and treadmills. There's a basic locker room. The current top-40 hits are pumping over the speakers.

But on closer inspection, you'll notice that there is actually a lot missing from this gym. There are no studios for yoga or spinning. There isn't a heavy-free-weight section. There aren't even any personal trainers. In fact, Planet Fitness forgoes many common gym features, such as:

- Towels
- A pool
- A basketball court
- Childcare
- Steam rooms, hot tubs, and saunas
- Free Wi-Fi

Even the typical gym-membership price tag is missing: while the average gym charges $52 a month, a basic Planet Fitness membership costs just $10.[1]

But Planet Fitness is not simply a story of a company trying to make a quick buck by slashing services and lowering prices. To understand the secret of Planet Fitness's success, we need to look at how lowering costs and simplifying services can be a deliberate innovation strategy—one whose aim is to make the fitness experience more satisfying to its customers, not less.

Planet Fitness members don't feel shortchanged by their bare-bones gym. They love that there are rows and rows of cardio machines, which means that they never have to wait to start their workout. And they don't miss the heavy weights: Planet Fitness's target customers don't care for those anyway. Lunch-time workouts are stress free without personal trainers trying to sell them services. The Planet Fitness model is cheaper to run than anything else on the market, but it still ranks first in customer satisfaction—even ahead of luxury giants like Equinox.[2] And the company keeps growing; at last count, Planet Fitness boasted over 7.3 million members working out in over 1,100 North American locations.

This is a company that has made careful, and sometimes difficult, choices to have a simple, low-cost offering. Along the way, it sacrificed temptations that lure other gym chains—such as personal trainers, a highly profitable add-on service that for most gyms brings in close to 10% of total revenue, or passive sources of income like rent from massage and physical therapists.[3]

Planet Fitness's success highlights an underappreciated approach to innovation: purposefully offering less as a way to satisfy more. Rather than trying to compete in the overcrowded luxury fitness field, with its lavish services and hefty price tags, Planet

Fitness found opportunity with a customer segment that most gyms rule out as unprofitable—casual and first-time exercisers. It then focused on a handful of things that these customers most prize, such as offering reliable workout equipment, with 24/7 access, at consistently low rates. That's all. The company chops out the usual profit-making mechanisms adored by the industry. It seeks customers most gyms avoid, because its low operating costs make those customers far more attractive to it than to rival chains. While the rest of the fitness industry continues to plow upmarket, Planet Fitness forges its own very successful path with a no-nonsense business model that delights its boardroom as much as its customers.

This is low-cost innovation, or costovation, hard at work.

What Is Costovation?

Costovation is a type of innovation that significantly compresses costs while still wowing customers. It's about *meeting* or *exceeding* customer expectations with *less*. Planet Fitness with its low costs and slim offerings—but ecstatic customers—is an example of costovation. Ryanair, an ultra-budget European airline which at one time tried to charge customers for drinking water and bath-room use, is not. The difference is in customer experience. Ry-anair tickets can be a grudge purchase, and purchases made with gritted teeth don't often lead to ever-thriving companies.

To get a better sense of costovation, let's look at an example from the hospitality industry. If you've ever been stuck on a six-hour layover, you know your options for comfort are bare: you can get in line for a shuttle to a local airport hotel (and plunk down your credit card for an entire night's stay), or you

What Is Costovation?

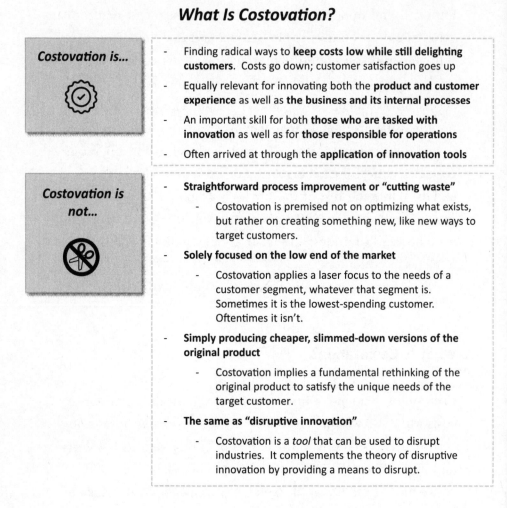

Costovation is...

- Finding radical ways to **keep costs low while still delighting customers**. Costs go down; customer satisfaction goes up
- Equally relevant for innovating both the **product and customer experience** as well as **the business and its internal processes**
- An important skill for both **those who are tasked with innovation** as well as for **those responsible for operations**
- Often arrived at through the **application of innovation tools**

Costovation is not...

- **Straightforward process improvement or "cutting waste"**
    - Costovation is premised not on optimizing what exists, but rather on creating something new, like new ways to target customers.
- **Solely focused on the low end of the market**
    - Costovation applies a laser focus to the needs of a customer segment, whatever that segment is. Sometimes it is the lowest-spending customer. Oftentimes it isn't.
- **Simply producing cheaper, slimmed-down versions of the original product**
    - Costovation implies a fundamental rethinking of the original product to satisfy the unique needs of the target customer.
- **The same as "disruptive innovation"**
    - Costovation is a *tool* that can be used to disrupt industries. It complements the theory of disruptive innovation by providing a means to disrupt.

can cozy up to a worn-out chair in the airport terminal. Both of those options are depressingly unappealing, especially for the frequent traveler. Enter Yotel.

Yotel is a hotel chain found in international airports like London's Heathrow and New York's JFK. Accommodations are often directly on-site within airport terminals, and rooms are extraordinarily small, fitting just a bed and an airplane-like bathroom.

But for time-conscious travelers, Yotel offers exactly what they crave—a comfortable bed, an excellent shower, strong Wi-Fi, proximity to their next flight, and fast check-in.

Yotel doesn't really offer much more than that, yet it's become quite popular with experienced travelers. This travel segment is not looking for extra amenities such as a tub, a gym, or a pool. And by keeping things simple, Yotel's back-end operations can be exceptionally lean. It uses automated kiosks for check-in and food vending, and it makes the most of its prime real estate by shrinking room sizes to tiny pod-like cabins. These cost savings enable Yotel to offer rooms that are much cheaper than a typical hotel—cheap enough that travelers use it during long layovers. At the same time, Yotel exceeds competitive offerings in critical ways, such as by providing monsoon showers for customers looking to de-grime after a long flight. Yotel runs a low-cost model, but it still nails the core needs of long-haul travelers looking for a quick place to rest and freshen up.

Many industries need a Yotel—a company that excels at offering something at a radically lower price, for a well-defined customer set. We've seen an increasing number of costovations in recent years, and as we'll soon see, they are often enviably simple in nature.

Innovation and Simplicity

Innovation is typically thought to mean *more:* more flavors, more options, more features. What makes costovation so radical is that it flips this understanding on its head and says that sometimes the winning approach is to do less.

McDonald's is a great example of how a less-is-more approach might have worked better. In 2004, the fast-food giant had 69 permanent items on its menu. A decade later, it had 145.[4] This 110% increase was rooted in a genuine desire to keep up with trends and give customers the variety they seemed to want. Diversifying its menu was an important part of McDonald's strategy to stay fresh, relevant, and exciting.

But expanding the menu so quickly added tremendous complexity to McDonald's operations. To accommodate the McWrap, for instance, supply-chain managers had to source a steady annual supply of 6 million pounds of English cucumbers (not an easy feat!). Staff that were used to assembling burgers had to be trained to make a McWrap and maneuver it into its specially designed container in under 60 seconds, with just the right amount of lettuce and chicken peeking out from the top.[5] Kitchen bottlenecks were further caused by limited-time-offerings items like Fish McBites, Steak & Egg Burritos, and White Chocolate Mochas. In 2013, Chief Operating Officer Tim Fenton told analysts that the chain had "overcomplicated" its menu by adding "too many new products, too fast. . . . We didn't give the restaurants a chance to breathe."[6] Two years later, McDonald's ran into the same problem again when it rolled out all-day breakfast, which cramped kitchen quarters as staff jostled to put an increasing number of food items onto limited grill space.[7]

Contrast that with Chipotle, a popular Mexican restaurant that McDonald's partially owned until 2006. Chipotle has offered virtually the same 25-ingredient menu since the company was founded over two decades ago. Customers mix and match these 25 ingredients to create custom meals, allowing Chipotle to win on freshness and personalization while also reducing complexity in its kitchens and in its supply chain.

Chipotle's strategy countered industry wisdom. The restaurant chain rejected limited-time offerings to boost sales and passed up low-risk/high-profit items such as coffee and cookies. They determinedly stuck to their modest menu and found a way to make it fresh and interesting to the everyday consumer. Despite its streamlined offerings, Chipotle is actually priced higher than McDonald's—showing that you can be upmarket, low-cost, and simple all at the same time.

Companies don't deliberately set out to make things complicated. But more often than not, they find themselves grappling with convoluted solutions to pressing problems that don't quite get them where they want to go. The mindset that "success is a function of doing more" so dominates how companies do business that going simple is rarely treated as a viable option. And, if paring things down does happen, it's typically through a cost-cutting campaign that has no innovation remit whatsoever.

Costovation defies this established thinking and suggests that big innovations can come from decluttering how you think, the way you do things, and what you offer. This book takes you through the nuts and bolts of how to costovate, and helps you decide when costovation is the right strategy for your organization.

Why Consider Costovation?

There are a lot of reasons why companies would want to costovate. Some are trying to surprise their competition or open up markets in industries that seem stale. Others use costovation to insulate themselves from the threat of disruptive innovation, or to build resilience against macroeconomic headwinds. Taking a birds-eye view of the field of costovation, here are three main reasons for why costovation repeatedly appears:

Cost-cutting is never easy, and there's no more fat to trim. Costovation is a different approach to cost-cutting. Here, cost-cutting is not the overall mandate, but rather a happy byproduct in the journey toward being truly customer-centric.

Why is this important? Companies have become extraordinarily adept at squeezing blood from stone, eliminating costs large and small whenever the mandate is given—often from areas such as administrative and operating budgets. But cost-cutting can only go so far. After years of this, there's likely little left to cut. In a 2016 study of 210 senior executives at U.S.-based Fortune 1000 companies, nearly half reported that they failed to meet their cost-reduction targets—a number that has climbed sharply from 27% in 2010 and 15% in 2008.[8]

The never-ending focus on cost-cutting and beating the industry cost curve—even when business is going well—has led to fatigue. We've heard again and again that companies need new ways to pursue transformative innovations in their operations. Costovation is one such solution.

Even in markets that feel saturated, there are still unmet needs everywhere. Although it can feel as though the world is cluttered with endless services and products, the reality is that many customers and businesses actually struggle with the products and solutions they use today. They complain about price, customer service, and the product itself; they MacGyver the products into more useful formulations. These customers will jump at opportunities to spend less if they can be well satisfied too. Costovation is a great tool for delivering on those needs.

Think of Airbnb. No one said the world needed another hotel company; there's a hotel out there for every kind of budget and taste. But Airbnb brought a different kind of lodging proposition—one that catered to unsatisfied desires for unique living experiences and for making easy money. Thousands of people who ordinarily would have stayed at hotels were delighted with the option to stay in a cozy, unique home. And thousands of people who would ordinarily have just let their spare bedrooms lie vacant were pleased to discover that they could generate income from them.

But even with Airbnb's meteoric rise to success, there are still countless unmet needs in hospitality that are yet to be satisfied—perhaps by the next great costovation.

There's a large swath of customers seeking low prices. Even during the long economic expansion of the past decade, many customers—both businesses and consumers—have struggled. For instance, despite a low unemployment rate of 4%, the average hourly earnings in the U.S. grew just 2.5% in 2017—which is hardly anything at all after accounting for inflation.[9] Many people are under constant pressure to make ends meet, and they need innovation relevant to them.

Moreover, we all know it is wise to be prepared for the worst, and recessions have not been abolished forever. Being prepared for macroeconomic downturns doesn't have to mean that you can't innovate and push forward. With costovation, you can do both.

Economies and industries can shift quickly, turning winners into losers seemingly overnight. Healthcare, for instance, used to pay high amounts for treating people when they were sick. Now, due to regulatory and economic pressures, the focus is increasingly on the opposite: paying low sums for keeping people healthy. The reversal has sent much of the industry scrambling, even while some early pioneers of this model like Kaiser Permanente are thriving in the new context.

While customer difficulties, economic downturns, and industry disruption may not be predictable, they are inevitable. Costovation enables nimble response.

What's Next?

The thesis of this book is that innovation and cost-cutting—so often considered magnetic opposites—can be a powerful duo, capable of reshaping markets and creating long-term competitive advantages. The backbone of our work comes from six years of research and analysis by ourselves and our colleagues at New Markets Advisors. We carefully investigated: *Are there patterns in costovation? How did these companies pull it off? And how can others do the same?*

We found that companies that excel at costovation share three traits, which form the core of Part II of this book:

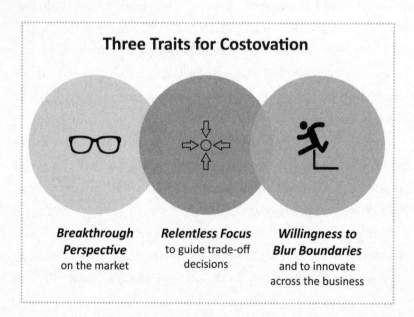

Three Traits for Costovation

Breakthrough Perspective on the market

Relentless Focus to guide trade-off decisions

Willingness to Blur Boundaries and to innovate across the business

TRAIT 1: Breakthrough perspective. These companies had a fresh perspective on the market. They threw out assumptions and long-standing industry beliefs and viewed their market and customers in a way that no one else had. The idea behind this is straightforward: the more unique your perspective on the market, the more you can differentiate yourself.

TRAIT 2: Relentless focus. The costovation winners have relentless focus. What they concentrated on could vary; for some it was a market segment, for others it was a customer's job to be done, and for still others it was a particular part of the business. But there was always a steadfast focus, just as in Planet Fitness's case. The focal points were critical for guiding the companies through the many decisions and trade-offs they had to make.

TRAIT 3: Willingness to blur boundaries. The most obvious place to innovate is on the product. But companies which excel at costovation—that is, the companies using costovation to shake up their markets—also took magnifying lenses to how their offerings were made, delivered, and sold. These companies innovated across different areas of the business.

————————

In Part III, we look at the mechanics of different costovation approaches. We delve into twenty costovation strategies—identifying what they are, when to use them, how they have been used in different contexts, and how you can get started.

Part IV is about the bigger picture. It provides a diagnostic for determining when costovation makes sense for an industry, examines how costovation fits into your broader business strategy, and finishes with a detailed checklist of how to begin.

Costovation is not a new thing, even if the business literature has largely ignored the phenomenon. Companies have been costovating for decades, and they have used established innovation techniques to help them get there. Our role has been to capture their learnings and show how to apply innovation methods toward a new goal: to wow customers with business processes and products that cost less.

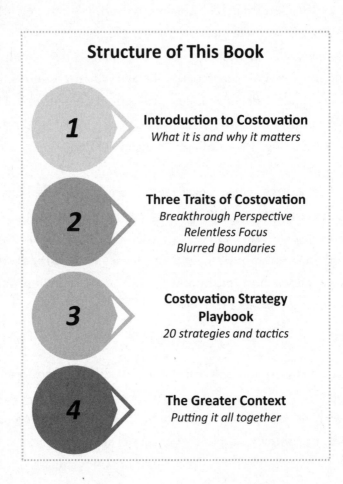

Structure of This Book

1 — **Introduction to Costovation**
What it is and why it matters

2 — **Three Traits of Costovation**
*Breakthrough Perspective
Relentless Focus
Blurred Boundaries*

3 — **Costovation Strategy Playbook**
20 strategies and tactics

4 — **The Greater Context**
Putting it all together

/ part two /

three traits of costovation

chapter 2

•

Breakthrough Perspective

In 2012, John Zimmer was running a carpooling startup with his best friend Logan Green when they asked themselves a fateful question: If we could do this all over again, how would we do it?

It wasn't that their company was failing. Actually, the opposite was true. Zimride—named not for Zimmer but for Zimbabwe, where the business idea was hatched—had grown at a steady clip in the 5 years since it was founded. It had coordinated carpools for tens of thousands of students at over 125 university campuses, saving a collective $50 million in vehicle-operating expenses. The website had $7.5 million in venture funding and 29 employees. It was turning a profit.

But the question still loomed over the Zimride founders' heads: What would we do if we were starting over today?

What was true in 2012 that had not been true in 2007?

Many things were of course different, but there was one trend in particular that would come to transform the Zimride founders' fortunes: the proliferation of smartphones. With smartphones, carpooling went from being something that you scheduled days in advance, to something that you hailed on demand—a revolutionary costovation that made transportation both cheaper *and* a better experience.

You likely haven't heard of Zimride, but you've certainly heard of Zimmer and Green's second company: Lyft. Five years after Zimmer and Green had their brainstorming session, Lyft was valued at $5.5 billion.[1]

Breakthrough innovation begins with breakthrough perspective. If you see the market in the same way that your competitors do, then you will solve problems in the same way that they do too. But if you can honestly answer tough questions—like the Lyft founders did about Zimride—you can discover seedlings of new opportunities that have only just broken ground. You can identify areas that are underserved and processes that are redundant. You can find weak points that are ripe for disruption.

This chapter is about how to defy the industry assumptions that so easily box us out of ground-breaking ideas, and how to develop a daring new perspective on your market. That's a precondition for every single costovation we've found, and it is key for long-term differentiation.

In this chapter, you will learn:

- Why breaking assumptions—and seeing the market and your business with fresh eyes—are core to cost-cutting innovation
- Five tried-and-true methods for developing a more unique perspective on your industry—and in the process, creating unexpected ways to approach your customers, market, and value chain

How We Get Trapped in Our Old Perspectives

One of Jennifer's first jobs was as an English-as-a-second-language teacher at a rural high school in Denmark. She was a young, nervous first-time teacher, keenly aware of the fact that she was scarcely older than her students. The lesson she had prepared was an English-teacher classic: the five-paragraph essay. It wasn't exactly creative—thousands of teachers had taught it before her, and thousands of teachers will teach it after her—but she thought it was a necessary part of her students' English education.

The lesson was going along better than she had expected—the classroom of eager students nodded along attentively—until she opened the floor to questions. And boy, did they have questions.

"Why does it have to be exactly five paragraphs? What do I do if I have a side point I want to make?"

"What if I don't have an argument I want to make?"

"Can my first paragraph be a question instead of a declarative statement?"

"We've never had to follow a writing formula before. Is this how Americans learn to write?"

Unbeknownst to Jennifer, Danish writing is more reflective and open-ended than the highly formulaic five-paragraph essay can handle. But before this encounter, she had never stopped to question the five-paragraph essay. It was just the way she had been taught. She herself had executed it dozens of times with reasonable success throughout high school. Jennifer might have officially been the teacher in that classroom, but her students were the ones giving her a lesson on how habit can lock us into tunnel vision.

If you have a young child—actually, if you've ever spent time with a young child—you know that humans are born questioners. But somewhere along the path to adulthood, we drop the questions, instead cocooning ourselves in confidence and all-knowingness. Then the fear of failure sets in, confining us to tried-and-proven approaches that are foolproof.

Businesses operate the same way. We pass down lore about the industry and the product category from generation to generation, usually under the labels of "prized company secret" or "commonsense knowledge about the industry." *The five-paragraph essay is an essential writing skill. You should arrange a carpool in advance over the web. A gym isn't a gym without a heavy-free-weight section.* Over time, these become set in concrete. And all it takes is for one company to shed outdated assumptions before the industry dominoes come tumbling down.

Shifting Perspective—Yes, Even in Large Companies

IN CLASSIC EXAMPLES of disruptive innovation, the winning underdogs are nimble startups that shake up old industries and products. But let's not pretend that being able to leverage critical perspective shifts is a tactic only available to scrappy entrepreneurs.

Take Toyota, one of the largest companies in the world. The post-recession years were a great time to be a car-company shareholder, with the industry buoyed by cheap gas prices, low interest rates, and sensational emerging technologies. Toyota was no different. In 2012, Toyota became the first automobile company in the world to produce more than 10 million vehicles per year. That same year, it also reported production of its 200-millionth vehicle ever. There was a lot to celebrate.

But while industry executives clinked glasses over the good times, Toyota was hardly lulling itself into complacency. In 2015, amid hot sales and record-high operating margins, Toyota announced plans to completely rethink the way it made cars.

"We are at a crossroads where we must now build a new business model," Toyota President Akio Toyoda solemnly announced. Toyota then laid out a new company mindset, one unbound by industry tradition: "We [want] to start from scratch to create the cars of our dreams, ignoring conventions and preconceptions."

Toyota's new approach to building cars involved massive behind-the-scenes simplification. Instead of designing new cars from the wheels up, Toyota decreed that future cars would be created from a single hyper-flexible base platform. Seat heights were limited to just 5 options. Basic components like steering wheels, pedals, seats, and radio controls were to be shared between models. All this meant that Toyota could build an entire library of models—from low-rise sport coupes to high-rise SUVs—without straying from a set of standardized components. And customers would be none the wiser: with everything covered up with nice fabrics and exteriors, the only difference they would notice was that they would be getting upgraded amenities for less.

Toyota's willingness to test industry assumptions gave way to a brilliant example of costovation. By shifting to a modular way of assembling cars, Toyota cut the cost of creating a new car by 20% and the startup costs of setting up a new production line by 50%. Future factories can be smaller and entirely single story, which saves on construction costs as well as heating and cooling bills. Magical numbers, indeed.

Five Methods for Developing a More Unique Perspective

Costovations defy assumptions about the way things should be done. This necessitates a different kind of thinking—one that dares to question.

If this sounds like something only "super-creatives" can do, you are luckily mistaken. For decades, behavioral scientists, thinkers, and inventors have sought to show that creativity and unconventional thinking are skills that can be learned. Our personal favorite among them is a Soviet man, Genrich Altshuller.

Altshuller, born in 1926, lived in a time when inventors were considered strange, eccentric people, like artists. They were thought to rise at odd hours, fueled by uncontrollable bursts of creativity. Their days would be punctuated by spicy mood swings. Their brilliance would come from glimpses of superhuman ability, or sometimes just accidents—either way, it was random.

But Altshuller was a serial inventor who didn't fit that mold. He was an early pioneer of the idea that creativity can be a *learned habit* for almost anybody, not just a divinely inspired ability granted to a select few. The Soviet regime liked that notion, although it also made sure some of his ideas didn't circulate too broadly (one of his early inventions, a method of escaping from an immobilized submarine without diving gear, was quickly classified as a Soviet military secret).

Over the next few decades, Altshuller developed a series of exercises that provoked creative thinking. He called it the Theory of Inventive Problem Solving, or TRIZ in the Russian acronym. While we assume that he would have preferred to work from his office or lab, many of his ideas were actually finessed in political prison, when Altshuller took an untimely detour to a Stalinist labor camp for "inventor's sabotage." This means that TRIZ was developed and tested in the most extreme of situations—during emergencies in the coal mine where Altshuller was assigned, for example, or in chilly prison cells where he brainstormed with other intellectual inmates—making it especially durable and practical.

We've adapted Altshuller's TRIZ methodologies into five lines of inquiry that can help you see your industry in a new light.

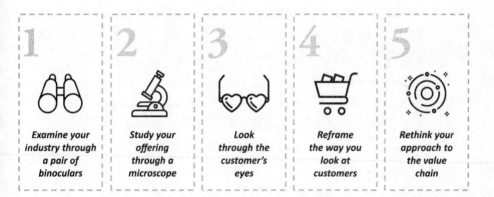

1	2	3	4	5
Examine your industry through a pair of binoculars	Study your offering through a microscope	Look through the customer's eyes	Reframe the way you look at customers	Rethink your approach to the value chain

1. **Examine your industry from afar, as if you're wearing binoculars.** Defy company and industry orthodoxy about your product and category.

The way things have always been done is not necessarily the best way to do them. Outdated ideas are grandfathered into industries all the time: restaurants shouldn't pass up high-margin add-ons like cookies, airlines must assign seating or there will be chaos, you need a license to taxi people around. No one intentionally drags old ideas into the future, but new forces—like breakthrough technology or reversed customer preferences—can prematurely age an idea. The key is in noticing when a long-held assumption is no longer true and acting upon it.

Avoid surprises from savvy competitors by continually reassessing how your industry has changed over time, and by questioning the relevance of long-held industry traditions. Make it a habit to step back from your industry and view it through the lens of someone who has laid eyes upon it for the first time.

For example, we'll wager that you haven't spent much time in the flower industry. So you'll probably be just as surprised as we were to discover that the "fresh" flowers that you buy at a supermarket or a boutique are actually two weeks old.

Two weeks—that's the amount of time it takes for flowers to be cut from a farm in Colombia or Ecuador, flown to Miami International Airport, wait for customs, be transported to giant refrigerated warehouses to be assembled into bouquets, and then put on trucks destined for floral shops and grocery stores all around the U.S. And that's if you're in the U.S.; if you're in Europe, your flowers have likely come two thousand miles from Kenya. By the time you see them, those flowers are extraordinarily well-traveled. They've exchanged hands with a dozen floral middlemen. And about half of them have gone to waste, having been broken out of dormancy prematurely by the slightest change in temperature.

No wonder cut flowers only have about a week's worth of life left in them by the time they land on your kitchen table.

In recent years, several startups have dreamt up solutions to this long and convoluted supply chain—new approaches made possible by fresh perspectives. For example, The Bouqs Company, a startup with $43 million in venture capital as of early 2017, scraps the majority of the floral supply chain, instead arranging for delivery directly from farmers to consumers. This eliminates the markup charged by wholesalers and retailers, and it shortens the amount of time that a flower spends stranded in a plane or warehouse rather than in a vase on your table. The result: cheaper flowers that last longer.

TRY THIS:

- List out 15 or 20 common assumptions about your product, category, and industry—the more basic and long-held, the better. Then consider what would happen if each assumption were suspended. What would be the pros and cons of this new configuration?

- Think through the history of your product, category, or industry, and compare it to today's state. How did we get to where we are today? Do the assumptions made in the past still hold true?

- Play with an idea you know is wrong and horrible. What makes it so horrible? Are those reasons well-founded? Are there small adjustments that you could make to that horrible idea that could disproportionately enhance it?

- Think about the customers you *hate* because it's so hard to make money from them. What are they really looking for? What don't they care about?

- Businesses—especially those that are blazing new trails— often do not take the most direct routes to where they are now. Knowing what you know now about your industry, is there anything you would change about your offering or organization? If you had to create your business again from scratch, what would you do differently this time around?

- Look at how your industry operates in other countries. There may be significant legal, political, and cultural differences that make drawing a strict analogy impossible, but keep an open mind about ideas that can be taken back home.

- It's also helpful to look to other industries for inspiration, since you are unlikely to happen upon truly breakthrough ideas by copying your competitors. Healthcare, for instance, can look to financial services, another heavily regulated industry. Don't reinvent the wheel—if there are good ideas outside your industry, draw inspiration from them.

2. **Study your offering through a microscope.** Question the little pieces—even the ones that have always been there.

Just as every industry is riddled with assumptions about how it works, there are also countless assumptions that are made about your offering. Break these apart by examining the details. Think of your offering as a management team; just as you would expect every member of the team to pull his or her weight, every part of your offering should contribute toward your company's mission statement and strategic objectives. There is tremendous opportunity in rethinking the details.

For example, take Jet.com, an e-commerce retailer acquired by Wal-Mart for $3.3 billion in 2016. Shoppers view it as a low-priced alternative to Amazon, but its brilliance comes from recruiting the customer to help with reducing costs along its supply chain. Prices reduce as you add more to your cart. Even more discounts are added if you add an item that is located at the same distribution center, since co-location makes the order cheaper for Jet.com to collect and ship. The site prices items according to your distance from their distribution center. You can save even more money by using a debit card rather than a credit card, or by waiving your right to free returns. By questioning individual pieces of the online shopping experience (and narrowing in on the ones that are most costly), Jet.com was able to be extraordinarily creative in finding ways to cut costs, and in a way that customers were happy to contribute to as well.

TRY THIS:

- Consider what would happen if we eliminated 90% of the features in your offering. Is there a customer type or customer occasion that might find this stripped-down version even better?

- Study your offering with an eye toward redundancy. Are there similar parts that could be merged together?

- Take apart the pieces of your offering. Can you think of a new way to rearrange the pieces?

- Can you divide your offering into smaller pieces? What would the advantages and disadvantages of that be?

- Can you turn a drawback into a highlight?

- We often pay most attention to the most and least popular parts of our offerings—the ones that attract the most praise and the most complaints. Take a magnifying glass to the ones in between—the ones that could get grandfathered into subsequent versions without critical review—and ask why, what if, and how. Do customers like this piece? Do they even notice it? Why has it gone under the radar? What if it were omitted? How could it be improved?

3. **Look through the customer's eyes.** Follow the journey of your customers' experience with your business, through their eyes only.

■

We often find that companies spend an inordinately small amount of time considering their offering from the customer's point of view. In their defense, it is easy to be fixated by back-end and internal issues. But having this disconnect between company and customer is dangerous.

Battle this by focusing first on the customer, and then designing products and systems around them and their needs. Customer-centric companies create innovations that resonate because they truly empathize with their customers and how they interact with the product category.

For instance, most cellphone carriers gear their services toward premium, high-use subscribers, providing them with expansive data and cell service, the latest in phone technology, and complicated contracts to match. But overlooked by this approach are casual users who don't use their phones often, yet still very much want to stay connected—for example, seniors.

Consider Consumer Cellular, one of Oregon's fastest-growing companies, where the average age of a customer is 63. Consumer Cellular does a terrific job of looking at phone technology through a senior's eyes. It offers simple pricing: a no-contract plan for around $25 a month, with no peak pricing or out-of-network charges. To ensure accessibility, the company works with phone manufacturers to pare down the preloaded apps, simplify instructions, and offer senior-friendly phones with larger buttons and hearing-aid compatibility. To ensure that the seniors receive the customer support they need, the company prioritizes U.S.-based call centers, and staffs them with representatives trained to work with customers who may be less tech-savvy or need more time.[2] Telecom is a commonly maligned industry, but Consumer Cellular shows how a company can be customer-centric and low-cost at the same time.

TRY THIS:

- Map out the entire customer journey for your organization, indicating every step or action that a customer might make to learn about your offerings, purchase them, use them, fix them, and dispose of them. Then do the same for the industry at large. What do you find surprising? Which steps can be challenging?

- Examine the *day-to-day* life of your offering. What pain points do customers experience? What can you do to alleviate those?

- Think through the *lifetime* of your offering. Where are the weakest points, such as in terms of product performance or customer service? What can you do to ease those issues?

- How have customers used your offering in unintended ways? What needs are they scratching at, and why are they using your offering to do so?

4. **Reframe the way you look at your customers.** Instead of looking at them in terms of demographics, try organizing them by the jobs they are trying to get done in their lives.

                                    ■

What is your market? The vast majority of companies respond to this question in terms of demographics: gender, age, location, educational levels, income, family size, occupation, race, marital status. *White upper-middle class suburban moms. Millennial-aged, unmarried urban males. Empty-nesters living in the American south. Retail businesses with less than $10 million in revenue.* Your competitors are likely defining the market in similar terms as well.

There's a reason marketers have done it this way for decades: demographic criteria are easy to measure and target, and this approach works well in many cases. But the theme of this chapter—and costovation more generally—is to break away from the traditions that everyone else is following. And in doing so, you can more accurately address customer needs.

In the distilled-spirits industry, customer segmentation has usually revolved around demographic criteria like age and gender. But this didn't give useful insights into how groups of consumers actually behave, or when and why one drink was chosen over another. A late-twenties male, for instance, would understandably make very different drink choices when on a date versus when out at guys' night at the local bar.

Here's another approach. Consider creating segments around the jobs that customers are trying to get done in their lives. These jobs are the underlying motivations behind why customers choose certain products. When at a fancy restaurant on a date, a fellow's job could be impressing his companion with his beverage selection. When at the bar with his buddies, his job is having a good time while sticking to a budget. Both of those jobs beg for distinct solutions—and if a company can deliver on those, they will be undeniably customer-centric.

There are *huge* numbers of jobs to be done that lack solutions, or that are being under-satisfied with current solutions. Go out and solve them.

5. **Rethink the way your industry approaches suppliers and other members in the value chain.** Forge new interpretations of old relationships.

We have extolled the virtues of prioritizing customer needs, but of course customers are not the only participants in your organization's ecosystem. The fifth in this series of mental exercises is to dole out attention to other partners in your supply chain—the ones that are less often catered to, such as suppliers, manufacturers, and deliverers. Like customers, these partners have jobs to be done, and helping them solve their own business problems can be a win-win situation for all. Very few companies even remotely consider these possibilities.

This is best illustrated through an example. In this case, let's select bread. For decades, bread arrived at stores prepared and ready to sell. Grocers would take the bread straight from the loading dock to their bakery shelves, and that would be the end of the bread journey. Midway through the 20th century, savvy bread manufacturers created a new technique called parbaking. Parbaked loaves are half-baked and frozen. They travel hundreds of miles in their half-formed state in refrigerated trucks before grocery-store employees finish baking and packaging the loaves.

Activity	Example
Step 1: Establish what you will use the segmentation for.	A large food company sought to understand the jobs to be done that couples have around dinner. These findings would be used to develop new products that speak to their target customers' underlying motives.
Step 2: Articulate the causation you are seeking to understand.	After brainstorming, the team identified independent and dependent variables for their research: ○ *Independent variables*: Customer jobs to be done and contexts that would have a strong statistical relationship with the dependent variables. ○ *Dependent variables*: Household income, eating preferences, geographic location (e.g., urban vs. rural).
Step 3: Explore the broad landscape of the jobs customers are trying to get done in their lives. This can be elicited through qualitative interviews, focus groups, and ethnographic research. You might be interested in checking out our firm's previous book *Jobs to be Done: A Roadmap For Customer-Centered Innovation*.	The team conducted a number of qualitative interviews to learn about how couples planned for, prepared, ate, and cleaned up after dinner. Additionally, researchers embarked on ethnographies to a few interviewees' homes, where they observed dinnertime habits in action.
Step 4: You'll probably find dozens of jobs. Provide some organization by sorting them into emotional and functional jobs. Then group similar jobs together, identifying high-level jobs versus specific sub-jobs.	The research produced a lengthy list of jobs to be done, which were organized into functional and emotional jobs to be done. ○ *Functional jobs*: Eat healthy, stay within budget, spend less time on menial tasks like vegetable preparation. ○ *Emotional jobs*: Unwind and relax, bond with my partner, learn new cooking skills, try new foods.
Step 5: Assess how different contexts affect the importance of various jobs to be done. You may wish to capture demographic, behavioral, and attitudinal information.	It became clear that certain jobs were more important than others depending upon the situation. For busy working professionals, for example, it was more important to spend less time on menial tasks than to stick to a strict budget. They didn't want to completely eliminate the cooking process, though; cooking was still a time for bonding and talking about the day. The researchers took note of these observations, and verified them through a quantitative survey.
Step 6: Identify clusters of customers that behave, make decisions, and prioritize jobs in similar ways. If you have a large enough sample size to do so, you can use statistical methods, such as cluster and factor analysis, to ground the groups in data.	The team combed through its notes and data, looking to see if there were patterns in job prioritization among certain demographic groups. How did couples' jobs to be done change by age, location, time availability, and income? These formed the backbone of their job-based customer segments. They formatted their findings in a table that showed how people in different contexts prioritized different jobs to be done.

Step 7: Determine the so-what implications, and think carefully about how different customer segmentations and sets of jobs to be done lead to different product conclusions.
 	
Here's a final checklist:
- Segments should be mutually exclusive and collectively exhaustive. In other words, they should be non-overlapping and should cover the entire market.
- Each segment ideally is bound by specific demographic or other identifying information that will enable you to find it in the market.
- You should be able to articulate for each segment a story about what makes the segment tick and how you can reach those individuals. Robust segmentation answers questions like:
  ○ What do they need?
  ○ How do they behave?
  ○ Why do they act the way they do?
  ○ How are they best served?
  ○ How will they judge ideas?
  ○ How do they rate competitors?
	One such customer segment was aspirational cooks. These were young couples who, despite having little cooking knowledge, wanted to create meals that were special, nutritious, tasty, and budget-effective. They didn't have the kitchen tools or time for elaborate tutorials. Rather, they were looking for meals that came together with a modest amount of preparation, but which still honored their belief that dinnertime was a time for relaxing with their partner after a long day at work.

On the surface, it seems counterintuitive that grocery stores would agree to take on this new work, not to mention investing in ovens and hiring special bakery staff. But what made parbaked bread stand out is that it offered a unique value proposition for grocers thirsting for ways to differentiate themselves: freshly baked bread in their stores, all throughout the day, and without the labor costs of artisan bakers. Sometimes the bread-baking would create delectable smells that would waft throughout the bakery. Parbaked bread spoke to deeper customer preferences by demonstrating freshness in the store, making the bakery look visually interesting, and creating a welcoming experience. It turned out to be a great proposition for the grocers. Bread manufacturers won as well, since longer shelf life allows for less frequent deliveries and produces less waste.

This symbiotic new partnership between bread manufacturers and their retail customers was a brilliant differentiator that came about because of a willingness to rethink traditional vendor partnerships.

TRY THIS:

- Identify the major types of players in your value chain. This may include suppliers, manufacturers, distributors, warehouses, retailers, and brokers.

- For each type, think through the dynamics of their business. What are the jobs they try to get done? What pain points hinder their progress?

- Brainstorm ideas that could help the other members of your value chain—for example, making them more efficient, helping them carry less working capital, or becoming faster to respond.

CASE STUDY: Taking This New Perspective All the Way to the Bank

When asked why he robbed banks, the legendary burglar Willie Sutton reportedly quipped, "Because that's where the money is."

After all, what's a bank without cash?

Seems straightforward enough, unless you ask Capitec, an up-start bank in South Africa. Since it was founded in 2001, Capitec has pushed the banking industry to question its basic assumptions—including the primacy of cash.

It may sound like a fantastical vision, but it's actually a business model grounded in practicality. It turns out that cash operations are incredibly cumbersome for banks. You have to train people to handle and count it. You have to organize separate activities to transport it from bank to bank. On top of that, you have to protect it with armored vehicles and security personnel. Capitec recognized this, and laid down an extraordinary example of costovation: it decreed that cash would not be available at the teller counter. Instead, customers could withdraw their cash at ATMs, or at the check-out register of a number of national retailers.

By cutting cash operations, Capitec freed up tellers from the drudgeries of counting and safeguarding cash—cost savings that Capitec passed down to its customers in the form of lower fees. Customer service also improved; instead of counting bills, tellers were able to focus their efforts on customer service and solving issues that mattered, without heavy glass separating them from customers. And it turned out that the retailers in the cash-back program were more than happy to participate as well. They were always looking for ways to reduce the amount of cash—and therefore risk—in their systems.

Capitec started off in the low-end market, but it has since worked its way up to the middle and higher-income segments, capturing bread-and-butter customers that incumbent banks have profitably ruled for decades. The company isn't even twenty years old, yet it has become one of the biggest banks in a country where the main competitive field has been the same for centuries. It got there by seeing the industry in a different light and reconceiving the core functions of a retail bank.

BONUS CASE STUDY: How Capitec Segmented Its Customers by Jobs to Be Done to Deliver Another Costovation

For decades, bank marketing departments have defined their markets by customer income levels—the thinking is that a household with an income of $20,000 has different banking needs than a household with an income of $200,000. Capitec's founders, who came from the spirits industry, were quick to dismiss this as "traditional banking," and went in the other direction.

Instead of segmenting by income, Capitec created a marketing structure based around groups of customers with similar banking needs and concerns, such as young first-time bank users who are starting their first jobs. These users don't need complex financial products. They haven't developed ingrained-enough banking habits to care that they can't withdraw cash at the teller. What they do care about is low fees, and personalized attention when they need it.

Internalizing these customer insights, Capitec set up basic, easy-to-use accounts. It could have followed others in creating more complex account options to capture potential revenue, but that would overshoot what its basic customer needed to get his or her job done. Instead, Capitec championed this user group, making smart cuts that achieved the dual mission of becoming a low-fee bank and better serving its target segment.

Young and low-income banking customers are traditionally viewed as unprofitable, but Capitec saw them as future banking customers-in-training whose loyalty was yet to be won. And Capitec captured that loyalty by focusing on the jobs that these customers were trying to get done—a fresh approach in a market where the same-old had always been good enough.

———————

When you watch football on TV, you see football in the way that TV executives think is most exciting: all eyes on the ball, handed off from player to player. Occasionally you also get close-up angles that capture the athleticism and daringness of the players. We see the puff of breath frozen in the air, and the Gatorade bucket lifted over the coach's head.

But that's not what the coaches and players watch when they are back in the locker room talking strategy. What they examine is the bigger picture: video clips of all 22 players on the field, creating fluid formations that have been designed to surprise, trick, and attack. As any player or coach will tell you, sometimes the most interesting developments on the field are not where the ball is.

So don't get locked into just following the ball. Change up the norms in your industry. Break habits. Toss assumptions. Start from scratch. Dare to slice your customer base differently. Ask questions that haven't been asked before. Break from the herd. Remember: *same thinking, same results.*

You won't land on a breakthrough costovation through these exercises alone, but going against conventional thinking enables you to see the problem in new ways—ways that just might lead you to shake up your industry. What to do about that unique perspective—that is, how to focus your costovation efforts—is the subject of the next chapter.

CHAPTER SUMMARY

All costovations are rooted in having a unique perspective on the market, industry, or business. If you look at your industry or market in the same way that your competitors do, you'll approach the market in a similar way to theirs.

But how do you come to that unique perspective? For some, this is a moment of realization that comes out of the blue. For others, a bit of brainstorming can spark those ideas. Here are five lines of inquiry that we like in particular:

☞ Examine your industry from afar, as if you're wearing binoculars. Take a step back from your business and try to identify long-held assumptions about the industry that may no longer hold true—or that can be tested. Just because you have always done it that way doesn't mean it is the best way to do it.

☞ Study your offering through a microscope. Concentrate on the pieces individually, instead of the whole. Ensure that every piece of your offering contributes to your overall mission and strategic goals. You'd be surprised how much "stuff" gets grandfathered into companies.

☞ Look through your customer's eyes, instead of your own. Companies get bogged down with issues that the customer has no idea about—a shipping container held up in customs, a supplier that wants to renegotiate a contract, a new IT system that is taking forever to install. But that's not what the customer sees, and that's not what the customer cares about. Do your operations truly focus on what your customers care about?

☞ Reframe the way you view customers and customer segments. Instead of organizing market segments around traditional measures like demographic groups or product lines, dig deeper into the jobs that these customers are trying to get done. The result will be fundamentally customer-centric.

☞ Rethink the way you view suppliers and other parties in your value chain. They always say customers may be king, but they are not the only ones in your business ecosystem with jobs they are looking to get done. Explore how you can help other parties in your value chain do their jobs better— and in the process, strengthen your own business.

chapter 3

•

Relentless Focus: Zoom In!

Hiroaki Aoki, or Rocky for short, lived a dozen lives in one. He was in a rock-and-roll band before becoming an Olympic wrestler for Japan in the 1960s. Then he was a champion powerboat racer until a terrible crash under the Golden Gate Bridge. He was convicted of insider trading and married three times. At one point he founded an adult magazine that is still in circulation today. And near the end of his life, he fought a bitter lawsuit against four of his own children.

But despite all this, Rocky's most lasting legacy was in the restaurant business. He founded the wildly popular chain of Benihana restaurants, which introduced America to the flavors of Japanese cuisine . . . and made it okay for chefs to toss food at diners to catch with their mouths. And while he was doing so, he flipped the restaurant model inside out.

Rocky was not a trained chef, but he had a knack for entertainment and for doing things his own way. There were two aspects of his restaurants which were particularly creative. The first was space management. At his restaurants, chefs were not hidden in a kitchen in the back. Instead they came to the dining table to cook, showing off flashy knife skills and serving food to diners piping hot. This brilliantly eliminated the need for a conventional kitchen, leaving most of the restaurant to be filled with revenue-generating dining tables. In fact, just 22% of a Benihana restaurant is "back of house," compared to 30% in a standard restaurant.[1]

Rocky's second great insight was the power of a simple menu. He offered just three entrees, all basic, easily cooked, and crowd-pleasing: steak, chicken, and shrimp. He wasn't being stingy; his choices were actually grounded in his intuition about his customers. "Americans enjoy eating in exotic surroundings," Rocky famously quipped, "but [they] are deeply mistrustful of exotic foods." The seaweed, sea creatures, pungent soybeans, and raw preparations that form the cornerstones of the Japanese palate were simply overkill for Rocky's theme restaurant. With this simple menu, kitchen inventory was a breeze, waste was significantly reduced, and chefs were recruited for their entertainment skills rather than their cooking techniques.

And so, despite the fact that diners had a limited menu selection, despite the fact that they might share a table with strangers, and despite the noise and relative chaos in the dining room, Benihana became a classic in both American culture and in restaurant operations lore. The way Rocky handled the details—his relentless focus on streamlining kitchen operations—was what set him apart from his restaurant predecessors.

In the previous chapter, we discussed the power of taking a differentiated view of the market, which can illuminate opportunities to which others may be blind. Now we'll zoom into the tinkering, prioritization, and detailed trade-offs that companies like Benihana make as they move toward costovation.

In this chapter, you will learn:

- Why having a relentless focus—and a clear vision for your final goal—is vital for a costovation project
- How to use strong strategic objectives to keep your costovation efforts on track
- What other companies have chosen for their costovation focus—and what to choose as yours

What Are You Working Toward?

Costovation is about relentless prioritization. If you are trying to cut costs, you can't have it all—and you better have some *vision* and *consistency* in the way you prune. The "vision" part comes from having a clear strategic objective, or a clear business reason for pursuing this new project. The "consistency" part comes from choosing a focal point that you will make your tactical priority. Let's address each of these in turn.

PART 1: Setting a Vision with Strategic Objectives

The first step in any innovation project is to know where you are going. What are your business reasons for pursuing this new project? What are you working toward?

This sounds simple—overly basic, even. But we bring this up because you would be surprised at how often this is glossed over. Innovation is like a $100 bill: everyone wants it, but they all have different ideas about how best to use it. Some are trying to refresh product pipelines that have gone stale. Some are trying to outwit their competitors. Others are looking for a new way to expand globally. Some companies want all the above. And there are still others who don't really know what the end goal is, pointing hazily to someplace "better" than where they are now.

Clear and succinct strategic objectives are important because they will guide you through the difficult trade-offs and decisions inherent in any innovation project. When tantalizing distractions spring up—saltwater pools and cucumber water in your no-nonsense gym, for example—your strategic goals will keep you on track. When your innovation team expands and takes on new members, those strategic objectives will help ensure steadiness in your and your colleagues' actions. Having a simple, easy-to-understand strategic objective is important for any project, but it is essential for costovation if you're to satisfy the twin objectives of low cost and customer delight.

To show why, let's revisit Planet Fitness. In its quest to deliver cost-effective gyms, Planet Fitness undoubtedly had some decisions that were easier to make than others. *Should it have a pool?* Well, a pool will take up a lot of space, and is expensive to install and maintain. It plainly doesn't jibe with a low-cost mentality—so out it goes. *What about daycare?* That can be a liability and requires hiring special staff. Cross it off the list.

But other decisions were not so easy, like *can we dramatically reduce the free-weight section?* Or, *what happens if we don't offer private training?* These are harder to answer. After all, what kind of gym doesn't have squat racks and hundred-pound weights? If Planet Fitness hadn't had a crystal-clear strategic objective, then the exercise of designing the gym concept could easily have descended into arbitrariness. They could have cut all sorts of expensive features, but that could have been done in a way that made little sense—or was even annoying—to the customer.

Planet Fitness's strategic objective was to become the gym of choice for first-time or casual gym-goers. That's a fickle crowd—one that often feels out of place in a gym and may not be motivated to work out, especially if they have to wait for a cardio machine. To help make casual exercisers feel comfortable and productive, Planet Fitness needed to have more elliptical machines and treadmills than the usual gym. And as for the free-weight section—that could safely be trimmed because it is a low-traffic area that often intimidates first-time gym users. When Planet Fitness decided to dedicate the majority of its floor space to cardio machines—essentially making itself a cardio gym—it satisfied the needs of its core customer while simplifying its business and real estate footprint. Having a strong strategic focus will help you make similarly difficult decisions.

Examples of Using a Strategic Objective to Keep a Company on Track

- **American Express** set an objective of differentiating its credit-card loyalty programs in a cost-effective way. Competitors were fond of offering airline miles and hotel certificates, but those were not cheap (nor were they unique). Amex's solution was to create experience-based rewards, which they called Gold Card Events; these included perks like seats at a hot new musical or tickets to a popular concert. Customers loved that they could now access hard-to-come-by events (a plus for differentiation), and American Express loved that these events were cheaper to run than providing certificates (a win for cost-effectiveness).

- The investment company **Edward Jones** sought to increase long-term growth per adviser. To do so, they developed a unique configuration: its only profit center would be the individual financial adviser. Other activities—even investment banking—would serve as support functions and would not be held accountable for generating profit. By doing so, Edward Jones fully aligned its innovation with its strategic mission.

Drawing Boundaries Means Letting Go

Choosing certain strategic objectives means not choosing others. If you choose to compete on price, you may not be able to prioritize selection or speed. The online shoe empire Zappos, for example, competes not on price, but on customer service, offering perks like free overnight shipping to differentiate itself. It also resolved itself to the reality that it will not underbid its competitors, killing any temptations to engage in price wars.

Drawing boundaries around your innovation strategy necessitates making trade-offs. Use this to your advantage. The strategic trade-offs you choose to make are what distinguish you from the rest of the market.

Choosing Strategic Objectives

IF YOUR ORGANIZATION has identified an overarching strategic goal for your efforts, great: skip over to the next section. But if not, start by setting a few small, tangible strategic goals. These can evolve over time, but it's important that you have them before investing further resources into your innovation project.

Here are our recommendations for when you don't have a clear strategic direction around your innovation project:

1. Define why you are innovating and what it means to win. Is it to differentiate your organization in the marketplace? To forge new paths into an adjacent market? To box out your rivals via price?

   Then ask: how will you know if you have achieved your goal? Often the goal is quantitative ("Create a new $25 million business"), but it can also be qualitative ("Improve brand perception among the millennial generation"). If you can, identify both an end point and a time frame for reaching it—but don't put too much stock in it. As helpful as measurability can be, in many cases it is not practical to guess at what a realistic goal may be at this point.

2. Decide how and with whom you will win. How far will your innovation efforts go? Are you seeking to disrupt a product line, a business model, or a customer? Without clear guidelines here, companies stumble, either limiting their focus to a few pet projects, or over-ambitiously investing innovation attention in areas where the company is unwilling to make changes. Make sure you are clear on your innovation boundaries and understand what is and is not organizationally permissible.

3. Determine competitive advantages and what makes your firm distinctive. Identify strengths, assets, and tactics that could be used to outperform competitors. What can only your firm deliver? Why should customers choose your

product over others? But be careful here: don't let yourself be boxed in by traditional views of the playing field or of the competition. This is a starting point, not an end point. It shouldn't close down consideration of market needs and possible new business plays.

PART TWO: Choosing a Focal Area to Make Your Vision a Reality

Over time, businesses tend to add things, not subtract them. They notice their competitors offering chilled towels and invest in a few towel fridges themselves. Then come the juice bar and the rain showers. This strategy of continually one-upping your competitors may have payoffs in the short term, but over time has the tendency to create a competitive field where each player looks strikingly similar to the last. It only takes one smart company to unseat them all with a low-cost offering that satisfies the customer's core needs.

You can resist the natural gravitational pull of premiumization—and avoid random and strategically meaningless innovations—by articulating a clear focal point for your innovation project and rallying around it hard. Your focal point forms the roadmap for achieving your strategic objective.

The focal point itself can be many things. It could be a certain kind of customer, like casual exercisers, or even simply an attribute, such as convenience. In our research, we found that there are four major focal areas that costovation companies drilled in on, and we'll visit each in turn.

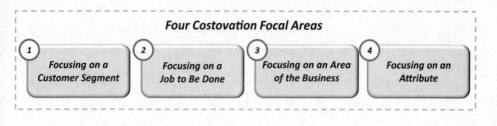

1. Focusing on a customer segment

The first focal point is a customer segment. This means championing a customer type and then designing an offering that satisfies its needs precisely—no more and no less.

Sometimes—but not always—the customer segment chosen is one that has been previously neglected. It might have been too small to warrant a tailored approach. It might have been unprofitable under the traditional business model. Or, the segment was neglected because competitors have been slow to respond to it—for example, a rapidly growing population or demographic.

In our introductory example, Planet Fitness chose to develop an offering designed for first-time and casual gym-goers. This is a customer group that traditional gyms struggle with; casual exercisers are hard to get in the door and prone to canceling their plans. But Planet Fitness created a gym experience that included just what casual exercisers needed—and nothing more—at a price point that they could tolerate even if they weren't good at sticking to a consistent workout schedule.

Focusing on a customer segment takes empathy and supreme listening skills. But tuning in to a customer's goals, aspirations, and jobs to be done is always, yes always, worthwhile.

EXAMPLES:

Customer segment: Budget-minded leisure travelers

Omenahotelli, a Scandinavian chain of hotels tailored for the budget traveler, guarantees just two things: a cheap rate and proximity to popular tourist spots. Anything else—like a lobby, receptionist, or even housekeeping services—is not part of the deal. Guests receive passcodes to unlock the front door, then self-service their way through their stay in highly standardized rooms. Omenahotelli runs on a simple concept—price and location above all.

Customer segment: Casual phone and Internet users

Free is a low-cost French Internet and mobile data provider. It does not try to provide the most reliable, highest-quality connections. Rather, it offers standard connections for customers whose data and mobile usage and performance requirements are low or average—for consistent, simple, and low prices. Free pulls this off by accessing existing networks (e.g., Orange) instead of building its own infrastructure. It targets low-maintenance users who are frustrated by variability and unpredictable pricing.

➤ ## How to Pick a Customer Segment

1. How big is the current potential of this segment? Market sizing is a critical tool here. The segment should command a large enough share of the customer population that it makes a targeted approach worthwhile in the first place.

ASK:

- What customer segments are not currently being targeted by the major players in your industry? How significantly sized are those segments?

- What are the "undesirable" or "traditionally unprofitable" segments? How big are they?

- What characteristics bind together those who do not consume any product in your category at all? How many "non-consumers" are there?

2. What is the growth potential of this segment? There's no way to be certain about the future, but trend analysis can give enough clues to inform your decision. Look for demographic shifts, trends in consumer preferences, legislative predictions, and potential new technologies. Conversely, keep an eye out for customer segments that may shrink in the future.

   ASK:

   - Which segments are forecast to grow, either due to demographic change or anticipated trends and discontinuities?

   - Examine your existing segments. Are they growing or shrinking over time?

3. What is the potential for disruption? Where are customers prone to opting for a less expensive, more accessible solution, even if it lacks performance on some dimensions, because existing options are too costly and cumbersome? These areas are prone to what's known as disruptive innovation.

Is your industry at risk of disruption? Questions to ask:

- Does the industry enjoy cushy profit margins? Are selling, general, and administrative expenses a large proportion of overall costs? Does a lot of money go to distribution or margins for sales-channel partners?

- Is there chronic customer frustration?

- Have prices for one segment increased faster than for other segments?

- Are some features of existing products not being used because they require too much skill, unusual need, or effort to access?

- Has there been a dearth of new competitive entrants?

- Where is there clear non-consumption of solutions because access is difficult or requires special skills?

4. Is there immediate fit? Is serving this particular segment feasible, given your company's capabilities, assets, and strategic goals?

   ASK:

   - Which segments have jobs to be done that are within your company's strategic objectives?

   - Where does your company have an unfair advantage compared to rivals?

There are very few "bad" focus areas; even shrinking customer segments in dying industries can be handsomely profitable as competitors close out of the business. What is more important is

true commitment to the segment that you pick. Businesses suc-
ceed or fail not through going after the wrong customer, but via
their judgment in how to serve those customers.

2. Focusing on a job to be done

A second area of focus for costovation efforts is around a job
that customers are trying to get done. Well-drawn customer
segments may be based partly on jobs to be done—like feeling
confident—but the job in and of itself is often too limited
a factor to constitute a true segment. Since jobs may cross
customer segments, focusing on them can enable access to a
broad set of customers without compromising coherence in
company objectives.

There are two major types of jobs to be done: functional
jobs ("de-grime after a long flight") and emotional ones
("feel good about my food choices"). Both are strong starting
points for costovation projects. Capitec zoomed in on the
functional job of storing money until it's needed. The bank
stripped away the complexities associated with traditional
banking to provide the simplest—and cheapest—banking
option for South Africans. On the other hand, Edward Jones
targets the emotional job of having peace of mind, in this
case through trusting a particular individual with financial
decisions.

EXAMPLES:

Emotional job to be done: Feel beautiful and confident

Take **Drybar,** a California-based chain of hair salons that
provides only blowouts—no haircuts, no color, no elaborate

chemical services. Women who pay around $40 for a blowout want to leave feeling beautiful and confident—that is their emotional job to be done. And Drybar hits the nail on the head: it decorates the space with happy, bright colors and plays feel-good romantic comedies with subtitles in the waiting area. It installed mirrors behind each chair, instead of in front; that way, there is a *wow!* moment when the stylist turns your chair around at the end of the blowout. Drybar is a habit for some women and a special treat for others, but all the details combined make it a place to go to feel glamorous and pampered.

Functional job to be done: Make use of unused commercial space

PivotDesk is an office-sharing marketplace in which companies or landlords can rent out extra office space to businesses that don't want to commit to a long-term lease. Pivot-Desk turns losses that were once unavoidable into financial opportunities.

Functional job to be done: Fill unsold hotel rooms

Hotel Tonight is a mobile travel app that helps hotels fill rooms that would have otherwise gone empty. People looking for "last-minute" reservations (generously defined as up to seven days in advance) can receive deep discounts on top-rated hotels.

How to Pick a Job to Be Done

1. Is it a high priority? Not all jobs are equally important—some are must-have's, others are great-if-possibles, and still others are sweet-but-not-a-deal-breakers. To sort between the jobs you're looking at, we recommend using quantitative research that forces respondents to rank their jobs to be done.

   ASK:

   - How do customers rank these jobs to be done? Are there some that are more important? What factors influence how important a job is?

   - How dissatisfied are people with their current ability to get these jobs done? How great are these pain points?

2. Is this opportunity large enough to pursue? Market sizing can be tricky because a single job to be done can span multiple distinct and sometimes non-obvious customer groups. But having a general sense of this opportunity size is critical information for deciding whether or not to hit "go."

   ASK:

   - Which customer types identify with this job to be done? How large is the market for each of those types?

   - What is the full range of competitors that are trying to address the same job? Consider all potential competitors—including those in different product categories or industries.

3. Focusing on an area of the business

Costovation can also be focused on a specific area of the business, such as procurement, order fulfillment, or post-sales customer support. Benihana, for instance, focused on making kitchen operations leaner and more cost-efficient, which it did by reducing the kitchen into a simple prep area and cutting the number of ingredients involved in the menu. Companies usually prioritize certain areas of the business based on what is perceived to have the greatest effect on achieving their strategic goals.

Some businesses are set up in ways that make this kind of innovation the most approachable for folks working in operations. If possible, we advise pairing this focus with a customer segment. Business operations are complex, and the innovation project can quickly revert to a cost-cutting project if you don't have concrete customer needs in mind.

EXAMPLES:

Area of the business: Inventory

Online children's clothing retailer **Primary.com** focuses on making it easy to replenish basic clothing like T-shirts that parents buy over and over again as kids grow. The clothing is gender-neutral, which cuts the number of unique items in half and creates enormous efficiencies in manufacturing and inventory management.

Area of the business: Installation

Concrete is traditionally expensive because you need a specialized cement truck to transport, mix, and pour it. **Cortex**

Composites—a maker of rollable concrete—focuses on easing the many pain points around concrete installation. The rollable concrete is sold in sheets and simply hardens when activated by water, making it four times faster to install at a savings of 30%. It is ideal in building situations where a thin layer of concrete is sufficient (e.g., drainage ditches, canal beds, patios, driveways).

Area of the business: Distribution

Warby Parker disrupted the eyewear industry with its vertically integrated business model. Instead of relying on retail partners to sell its products, Warby Parker distributes glasses through the postal system at great savings for its customers.

➤ ## How to Pick an Area of the Business

1. Which area of the business is traditionally the most expensive or cumbersome in your industry? A great place to start is by addressing the Achilles heel of your industry.

   ASK:

   • What would an outsider find most surprising about your industry?

   • Where in the business have your competitors focused their innovation efforts, if any?

2. Which area of the business creates the most pain points for your customers? Improving one part of the business can have an outsized impression on your customers' experience with your overall company.

ASK:

- What part of your offering do customers find the most trouble with? Does that map to any particular area of the business?

3. Is there more than just one area of opportunity? In some cases, it makes sense to bundle together multiple areas of the business (e.g., inventory and distribution together).

4. What will get off the ground fastest in your organization? There are political and structural reasons that can make one area of the business more fertile ground for innovation than others.

5. Look outside your industry. Where do you see operational innovation occurring? Sometimes innovation occurs in trends; the vertically integrated e-commerce model, for instance, is disrupting industries one by one. Pay attention to events in other industries that could foreshadow upcoming disruption.

ASK:

- Look at industries that are analogous to yours. Are there themes or trends in operational innovation?

4. Focusing on an attribute

A fourth area of focus is on an attribute, like speed or consistency. These are outcomes and goals that customers are seeking to meet—such as convenience, or price, or ability to customize.

This approach is a cousin of the job-to-be-done approach, which tends to be specifically focused on a customer segment.

EXAMPLES:

Attribute: Delivery convenience

Casper sells mid-range mattresses online, sparing customers from the stress of haggling with a mattress salesman or renting a truck to bring the mattress home. For a certain type of customer, Casper's offerings are incredibly convenient. But the trade-off is in selection: Casper offers only one level of firmness ("medium-firm"). A strict obedience to its strategic objectives—in this case, convenience for the millennial shopper—prevents extra features and extra complications from creeping into Casper's business.

Attribute: Price

GEICO's low-cost insurance model is premised on direct consumer marketing instead of the traditional relationship-based sales model, which involves training and employing costly agents. GEICO is a reputable company, but it doesn't overpromise: it doesn't advertise having the best service or offering the most complete coverage. It promises low rates and delivers just that.

Attribute: Speed

Pret A Manger is a self-serve café that caters to busy working professionals who need to grab food quickly and go. Pret speeds up the lunch experience by selling ready-made sandwiches and meals, which are assembled in the morning at high volumes and with a high degree of standardization. Customers help themselves as if at a supermarket and don't need to wait for preparation. The trade-off is in customization: Pret does not make to order.

Attribute: Customization

A new crop of schools, united under the venture capital-funded **Altschool** network, upends traditional notions of school: there are no roll calls, bells, distinctions between grade levels, secretaries, principals, lectures, or class periods. Instead, students are largely guided by a software program on a tablet that prompts modules based on student interests and needs. When students finish their task, project, or assignment, they move on to the next one, at their own pace. In this school, teachers follow the natural interests of their students, not the other way around—part of Altschool's commitment to individualized education. Tuition comes out to ten or twenty percent less than private school tuition, in large part due to the fact that administrative and technical needs are managed centrally, leaving each school to simply be staffed by teachers. The school zooms in on a single driver—providing the best in personalized learning—and discards other parts of the traditional school that do not directly contribute.

Attribute: Ease of maintenance

NYC-based startup **Priority Bicycles'** quest was to create a cheap, maintenance-free bike. To do so, it put every piece of the bicycle on trial, testing its durability. Hand brakes, for example, are one of the most common repairs needed on a bike, so Priority eliminated them. They substituted a simple foot brake that could go thousands of miles and many years without needing service.

→ ## Tips for Picking an Attribute

1. Pay attention to attributes that are considered secondary or tertiary in your business. While the rest of the competition fights over marquee features—like cost—see how you can differentiate your strategy by excelling on secondary (but still valuable) attributes.

2. What do customers consider the main pain points for your category? This could be any pain point at any point in the lifetime of the product. Articulating this can clue you in to the attributes that can be real differentiators in customers' eyes.

3. Understand how an attribute can vary throughout your customer base. Attributes can mean different things to different customer segments. Use market-research techniques to assess how important an attribute is and when it matters most.

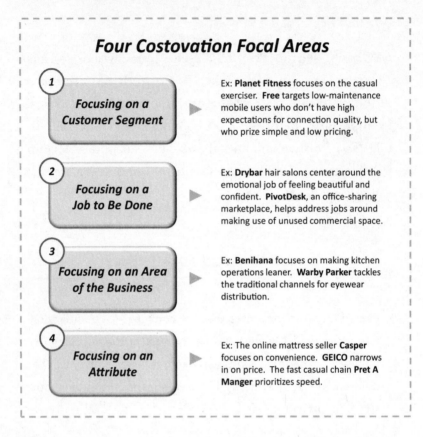

Four Costovation Focal Areas

1

Focusing on a Customer Segment

Ex: **Planet Fitness** focuses on the casual exerciser. **Free** targets low-maintenance mobile users who don't have high expectations for connection quality, but who prize simple and low pricing.

2

Focusing on a Job to Be Done

Ex: **Drybar** hair salons center around the emotional job of feeling beautiful and confident. **PivotDesk**, an office-sharing marketplace, helps address jobs around making use of unused commercial space.

3

Focusing on an Area of the Business

Ex: **Benihana** focuses on making kitchen operations leaner. **Warby Parker** tackles the traditional channels for eyewear distribution.

4

Focusing on an Attribute

Ex: The online mattress seller **Casper** focuses on convenience. **GEICO** narrows in on price. The fast casual chain **Pret A Manger** prioritizes speed.

As we've mentioned, these four categories are not mutually exclusive. You don't have to pick just one, and in fact some drivers work better together. Benihana, for instance, focused just as much on its back-end operations as it did on catering to the entertainment needs of families and birthday parties. Together, these foci worked together to make its model truly compelling.

The important thing is that you pick one or two and stick to them. Zoom in! Costovation requires choice.

How to Pick a Focus

Of the four categories we've laid out, and the countless possibilities within each, how dp you know what particular area to concentrate on? Here are several indications to keep in mind as you determine your focus:

Customer Segment

- You are keen to deliver excellent *customer experience* for a target population
- There are overlooked segments in the customer population
- There are distinct segments which will grow, due to demographic shifts or trends
- There are a variety of jobs to be done that you wish to address together

Job to Be Done

- You've identified an under-satisfied job to be done that spans multiple customer groups and demographics
- The projected population is large enough to justify a unique venture there

Area of the Business

- You have a clear idea where within the business or organization major costs come from
- Your organization is structured such that operational innovation will be most effectively executed by those working in specific operational areas

Attribute

- You are driven by a strong value-based mission statement or vision that does not specify a particular customer group
- You have identified an attribute that is highly valued by users and yet is under-capitalized on by industry participants

CHAPTER SUMMARY

All costovations feature a relentless focus, and a willingness to make trade-offs in the name of that objective.

In order to narrow down what you concentrate on, you need to know your strategic mission. A surprising number of companies don't have clear goals for their innovation programs, instead adopting an "I'll take whatever I can get" mentality. But it's important to know where you are intending to go, and how you'll know when you've gotten there. Having a crisp strategic statement will help you stay on track. It will give you long-term vision and consistency.

There are a number of options for what your costovation focus can be:

☞ A customer segment

☞ A job to be done

☞ A certain part of the business

☞ An aspirational attribute

☞ A combination of the above

Use your strategic objectives to help you select a focal area, and make it your North Star when you are forced to make trade-offs and difficult decisions about the direction of your costovation initiative.

chapter 4

•

Willingness to Blur Boundaries: Innovating Beneath the Surface

In 2003, residents of the city of Denver were abuzz about a mysterious man they knew only as Ted. It started when hundreds of flowers were delivered to Denver hospitals with cards signed "Ted." Then Ted treated a restaurant full of diners to dessert. Not long after, an unfamiliar marching band was spotted at local sporting events, inexplicably chanting "Go, Ted!"

The suspense only grew. Passengers in planes flying in and out of Denver International Airport noticed that the letters T-E-D were spelled out in huge sod lettering on a local farmer's land. Blue-and-orange "Ted" stickers appeared at a Broncos game. Paid actors wearing sandwich boards teasing "I'm not Ted" loitered around downtown. *Who in the world was Ted, and why was he being so coy?*

Ted turned out to be United Airlines' new low-cost carrier, an airline-within-an-airline built to battle the rise of discount liners like Southwest. Ted was based on the oldest strategy in business: if you can't beat them, copy them.

Ted had all the familiar trappings of a low-cost carrier. It had a single-class cabin, reduced legroom, and no free snacks. Instead of charging twelve or fourteen different fare classes, Ted had just six. It flew to leisure and secondary markets such as Miami, New Orleans, and Las Vegas, none of which competed with United's premium routes. It used a low-cost guerilla marketing spectacle to publicize its quirky personality. United, fresh from declaring Chapter 11 bankruptcy, pinned its hopes for recovery on this new darling.

But it soon became apparent that Ted's cost innovations were superficial, like coats of new paint on a crumbling wall. While the new discount liner was flashy from a marketing standpoint, relatively little effort was put into process innovation—with the result that the costs of flying a Ted plane were not much different than the costs of flying a regular United flight. The same people who flew and serviced United planes were the ones who flew and serviced Ted planes. Last-minute equipment substitutions meant that in many cases the planes were the same too. Ted tickets were sold through traditional channels, meaning that United continued to pay commission fees on them.

Ted was designed to imitate the breakthrough innovations that had enabled Southwest Airlines to soar. But in reality, Ted had only copied Southwest's most visible, surface-level innovations. Southwest had done far more than just eliminate the First Class section and assigned seating: It pioneered new productivity-raising labor practices, such as having flight attendants clean the lavatories during aircraft turns, and making baggage handlers responsible for aircraft pushback. It minimized its maintenance and training costs by using a fleet of just one kind of aircraft. It made it a priority to cut down on the amount of time a plane wasted waiting on the tarmac in between flights. It flew short routes where reduced time on the ground had the biggest impact on overall plane utilization.[1]

And so, when fuel prices skyrocketed in 2008, what little cost savings Ted had achieved were overwhelmed. Without true operational innovation to support the business, Ted was unable to replicate Southwest's success. It folded in early 2009.

Innovations that come from the revenue side, like Ted, are often the loudest. These are the projects that end up in magazine features and TV interviews, because customer appeal is fundamental to their success. But costovations, or innovations from the cost side, can't be underestimated. They can be sly and disruptive, secret weapons that can sneak up on the market when no one is watching. And when the competition notices what is happening, they are stunned to find that costovations can be much, much harder to copy.

In Chapter 2, we discussed how the key to breakthrough costovation is having a unique perspective on the market. In Chapter 3, we zoomed in on the attitude of disciplined focus in which costovations are rooted. Now, in the final chapter of this section, we'll dig into the innovation mechanics that happen deep inside a business and point out areas where costovation opportunities are particularly abundant.

In this chapter, you will learn:

- How much opportunity there is to innovate in ways that don't just result in a new version of your current offering
- The five areas of your business where costovation opportunities are particularly rich

- How multiple simultaneous innovations can work together in concert

Operational Innovation Done Right

For many companies, innovation is product-oriented. This
means that innovation efforts almost always result in a shiny new
offering that we can see and touch, like new menu offerings or
next-generation car models. Sadly, many of these new products
are unlikely to materially change a company's growth trajectory:
Nielsen estimates that for every 100 new fast-moving consumer
good products launched, 85 fail in the marketplace.[2]

The kind of innovation that we usually think of when we think
of "innovation" is just the tip of the iceberg. The goal of this
chapter is to illuminate the rest of the iceberg—because under-
neath the surface, there are enormous opportunities for operational innovation that can have profound and lasting impacts on
the bottom line.

Take a look at Starbucks, for example. Starbucks was an early
explorer of what an "omnichannel experience" could be for an
industry based on brick-and-mortar stores. Its Mobile Order &
Pay program—tested in December 2014 in Portland, Oregon,
and implemented nationwide nine months later—was a quick
win for both the customer and the company. Using the Starbucks app, customers order and pay for their drinks on their
phones; a few minutes later, they are free to walk into their
Starbucks store, skip the line, immediately pick up their drink,
and be on their way. This shaves precious time off a harried
morning commute and automates a process that is repetitive
and predictable.

For Starbucks operations, the upside is even greater. Mobile ordering reduces the staffing needed at the register, freeing up baristas to make drinks—the real money-making part of the business. It also gives them more time to connect with customers. Lines become shorter for casual, walk-in customers who would otherwise be intimidated by large crowds, which increases overall foot traffic. Mobile ordering increases the number of orders that a store can accept per minute, making each store even more productive.[3] And payments on the Starbucks app are made with pre-loaded gift card-equivalents, encouraging frequent visits and increased loyalty.

Starbucks, like many companies, is no stranger to incremental innovation—its 87,000 possible beverage combinations are a testament to that. But mobile ordering was a deeper kind of innovation that rewired in-store dynamics. It was a completely new way of paying for and filling orders, changing the way customers interact with the brand. And this operational innovation made a big impact on the business: just over a year after Mobile Order & Pay was rolled out, 7% of all purchases in company-owned U.S. stores were ordered ahead, and over 1,200 stores reported 20% or more order-ahead transactions during peak times.[4] In spring 2017, Starbucks announced that it would test a mobile-only store in its Seattle headquarters.

> ## Notable Operational Innovations You'll Recognize
>
> - **Code-share agreements between airlines.** Selling extra seats to other airlines helps cover operating costs and ensures that a seat never has to fly empty. The sharing economy may be a hot topic now, but airline code-sharing presaged it by four decades.
>
> - **Ambulatory surgical centers.** These surgery clinics, where patients are in and out in the same day, have surged in popularity in the past two decades. Patients say they get better customer service at a lower price point—a feat made possible by eliminating money-losing departments such as the emergency room and focusing services around the more profitable operating room.
>
> - **Drive-through lanes at fast-food restaurants.** Going through the drive-through is a gift of convenience for customers, who can receive orders within minutes. The restaurants benefit from quicker customer turnaround and the ability to decrease the seating area required.

Five Places to Look for Operational Innovation

In traditional product-oriented innovation, marketing or R&D comes up with the ideas and operations executes. In costovation, operations can be the instigator, a true partner in innovation. As you grow your business, consider how you can apply innovation ideas to not just the visible parts of the business that are floating above water, but also to the rest of the iceberg below. Every part of the business can be fertile ground for innovation.

Here are five areas of the business where costovation opportunities are particularly rich—illustrated for simplicity with examples from the retail industry.

1. Costovation in the product itself

The most common interpretation of "innovation" is something new in your offering—whether that is a product or a service, or both. Product innovation is splashy and visible, making it easier to get customers excited and stakeholders on board. It is also the easiest to copy.

Costovation in the offering itself can take many shapes. Common themes include *simplification* (often to target a specific customer category's needs) and *technological enable-ment*, which uses new advances in technology to address customer needs in ways that were previously impossible.

How Costco used bulk sales to bring discounted, quality goods to small business owners

Before Costco, bulk discounts were a privilege limited to business customers that were large enough to make use of several pallets of paper towels at once. Costco's contribution to the retail industry was in making bulk purchasing accessible—this time to small business owners, large families, and anyone else who was willing to pay a modest yearly membership fee. It was an unusual idea with an untested business model.

To ensure sustainability in the business, Costco's trade-off was a de-emphasis on selection, which simplified inventory management and back-end logistics. And since the small bulk packages were unique in the market, manufacturers could sell their goods to Costco at low prices without fearing that consumers would easily compare prices with other retailers and demand across-the-board price-cutting. Costco lowered prices while delighting its customers with a store that catered to their needs—a great example of costovation in the core offering.

2. Costovation in how the product is made

■

This is where we get into the details of manufacturing and assembly. Costovations in this realm help companies make giant steps in the way they make their product—often to make production faster, cheaper, more flexible, and easier to customize. *Postponement* (making customization more efficient by delaying it for as long as possible), *modularization* (accelerating build time by working in chunks), and *external innovation* (companies working together to create something new) all find their home here—along with redesigned factory floors, interlocking pieces in the final product, and new manufacturing techniques.

How Trader Joe's used private-label products to both cut costs and deliver experiences that customers couldn't find anywhere else

Trader Joe's is known for low prices and a cheeky sense of humor, but what brings customers back again and again is its "destination products" that shoppers can't buy anywhere else. Some of those products are developed in-house; a great many, however, are results of collaborations with its manufacturers and suppliers to create private-label products. This way, Trader Joe's shifts a portion of R&D costs to its partners, while also harnessing their creativity and market insight. Trader Joe's wins in the speed department as well, since supplier-led innovation often makes product development faster and more cost-efficient.[5]

3. Costovation in how the product is delivered

■

The third area to probe for costovation opportunities is in how your product is moved. This includes everything from how the distribution chain is arranged to improvements in the transportation methods themselves. Costovations in this area tend to fall into three categories: a better way to do what you do now (e.g., leveraging technology or partners); a fundamentally new way to do what you do now (e.g., leapfrogging usual distribution steps); and a forward-looking action plan for answering the big distribution trends of tomorrow (e.g., distribution systems designed for the unique constraints and infrastructure of super-dense megacities in emerging markets).

How Wayfair eliminated its warehouses

Wayfair is an e-commerce furniture seller that made over $4.3 billion in sales in 2017. Furniture is heavy, but the company created a business model that is extraordinarily asset-light. Unlike Overstock or Amazon, Wayfair doesn't touch most of the products it sells. It doesn't manage a huge network of distribution centers or dozens of warehouses full of sofas and bed frames. Instead, Wayfair manages a website—a great, user-friendly one with elaborate search options such as by room, furniture type, color, life stage (e.g., adult, teen, kid), gender, and level of care (e.g., machine-washable bedding versus dry-clean only). Once a sale has been made on the website, Wayfair leaves it to manufacturers to ship purchases directly to the customer.

Inventory is usually a major drain on a retailer's working capital, but Wayfair's asset-light model has enabled the company to grow its business at astounding rates, including in Europe where it has little physical presence. It has completely re-envisioned what a furniture company's distribution system looks like.

4. Costovation in how the product is sold

∎

Fourth, don't overlook innovating the way you sell. Unlike previous categories in this list, the sales process is a fundamentally

customer-facing action. It is a critical part of the overall customer experience and begins the moment the customer
learns of your company or product name. Costovations in this
area could include new ways to handle payments, innovations
in the pricing model, and new ways to deploy the sales department. It can also involve new ways for customers to interact
with a brand throughout the buying process.

*How Indochino made custom suits affordable with its "traveling
tailor" approach*

Indochino sells custom suits at a 50% discount, which is made
possible by the fact that the measuring and ordering process
is moved online. Without the burden of a brick-and-mortar
store (or even inventory, for that matter), the brand can com-
fortably strip out the traditional mark-up around suits. Instead
of employing full-time store associates to take measurements
and wait around for customers to show up, Indochino sends
a small number of "traveling tailors" to major cities around
the U.S. for weeks at a time. Customers can schedule free,
15-minute measuring appointments with the traveling tailors—or they can take the measurements themselves by following an online step-by-step tutorial. Indochino's creative response to the custom-suit arena has been especially well taken
up by a young, millennial generation of men buying their first
set of professional suits. The service forsakes the traditional
second fitting that is common in custom-made suits, which
enables fine-tuning of measurements, but in doing so it at-
tains massive cost advantages.

5. Costovation in how the business partners with its ecosystem

Though many businesses exude an "us-versus-them" mentality, the fact is that they don't operate alone. They instead live in rich, lively networks, full of suppliers, vendors, and other partners. Our view is that each one of those relationships represents an opportunity for symbiosis, such as asset-sharing. When your vendors and partners are strong, you are too.

Due to their partnership nature, costovations that leverage ecosystems are sometimes more difficult to pull off. But they can also be the most impactful on the industry, with effects that ripple throughout the network. Start small with one or two partnerships, and build up from there.

How Amazon moved in with P&G to lower the cost of shipping

When it comes to buying bulky household staples like paper towels and diapers online, the cost of shipping can be a major hurdle. In 2010, Amazon sought a way to make it more financially reasonable—by moving into a P&G warehouse in Pennsylvania. Now, when an order is placed, products move straight from the warehouse shelf and into an Amazon employee's hands, where it is promptly packaged, labeled, and shipped away. This speeds up shipping time and lowers transportation expenses for P&G. Amazon benefits from not needing to store bulky, inexpensive items in its precious warehouse space.[6]

Nurturing its ecosystem of partners helped Amazon discover synergies in unexpected places—a model that Amazon now practices in seven P&G distribution centers around the world. Other manufacturer partners such as Seventh Generation, Kimberly-Clark, and Georgia Pacific are following suit.

Multiple Innovations Working Simultaneously

A small number of companies manage to innovate not just in one category but in multiple ones simultaneously, bringing to market transformative new solutions.

For example, let's look at Picard, a popular grocery retailer in France that sells only frozen food. Freezer meals have a less-than-savory image in the U.S., but Picard's offerings are gourmet—think dishes like Basque chicken, vegetable tartine, and specialty sausages with morel mushrooms. Customers rave about having Picard products on hand for an easy dinner party, for a quick work lunch that still feels elegant, or for a wholesome meal when you're too tired to cook or go out to eat. Pricing is higher than a typical frozen pizza, but far less than the cost of having the same meal at a restaurant, which is what Picard has targeted as its true competition. Picard is so beloved in France that in 2014, French consumers ranked Picard as their favorite brand, in a land with no shortage of appealing brands.[7]

Picard's food may be fancy, but everything else about the operation is exceptionally lean. Stores are tucked into tiny spaces—helping the company save on real estate. Since they are so compact—usually just one or two aisles—they only need a couple employees at a time, creating massive labor savings. The number of unique items within a single store is insanely low (400 compared to 150,000 at Walmart)—which drastically simplifies inventory management. Since all of Picard's food is frozen, inventory is less perishable, and packaging can be optimized for shipping—meaning Picard leaves no money on the table with regard to distribution.

How many types of innovation did Picard bake into its business model? At least four, by our count:

1. **Product:** Picard sells only frozen food. This greatly limits the number of unique items it has to handle.

2. **Make:** Products are private label, meaning that Picard can skirt around distribution brokers, brand management, and other sources of overhead costs.

3. **Deliver:** Twice-daily deliveries enable stores to practically eliminate the stock room, meaning that more store real estate can be put toward customer-facing uses.

4. **Sell:** Picard stores are small and tucked into urban areas. The small store footprint means that Picard can hire fewer staff, and shoppers can easily find what they are looking for.

The result is a business model that is difficult to copy, which is invaluable when you're competing in an industry as competitive and unforgiving as grocery. Layering multiple innovations also enables Picard to forge its own pricing standards and refrain from price wars, since it creates new forms of value and offers a combination of convenience and quality that was previously unmatched in the market.

Innovating across several areas of the business can be much harder to execute than a singular innovation. On the flip side, it opens up possibilities to redefine not just product lines, but entire playing fields.

The Three Costovation Traits in Practice

Education in Kenya is a story of two extremes: Public schools are crowded and understaffed; they are supposed to be free, but parents often pay bribes to keep their children in school; and half of all public-school teachers play hooky.[8] Private schools, on the other hand, can cost as much as tens of thousands of dollars a year—an exorbitant amount for a country where the average monthly wage hovers around $76.[9]

Bridge International Academies—which just celebrated its tenth year—creates a third option between ineffective public schools and unaffordable private ones in Kenya. Its solution is a chain of low-cost private schools where tuition is priced at a headline-grabbing $6 per month.

Six dollars a month for quality, private education is a feat in any market. Bridge's singular goal was to radically decrease the cost of education, and it used highly creative means to make it possible. Lesson planning, for instance, is one of the most time-consuming parts of teaching—so the Boston headquarters develops curriculum and scripted lessons, which teachers in Kenya deliver with the help of a tablet. To cut down on overhead, each Bridge school has only one administrative staff member, and he or she runs the school through a smartphone connected to a central cloud-based server. The physical school buildings are built in just one month, using one of three design templates. The cost to families is still a sizable expense for the poorest attendees, but a much better value than the alternatives.

This might sound like a unique one-off school, but the reality is far from that. Bridge counts over 520 nursery and primary schools in its portfolio, and its lessons now reach over 100,000 elementary-aged schoolchildren across Africa and Asia every day. Since it was founded in 2008, Bridge has attracted hundreds of millions of dollars from high-profile investors such as Bill Gates, the Chan Zuckerberg Initiative, and eBay founder Pierre Omidyar.

Let's break down this example into its three core costovation traits:

COSTOVATION TRAIT #1: Breakthrough Perspective. Bridge's costovation is rooted in its daringness to question the traditions that we have assumed to be integral to schools. Instead of having teachers reinvent the wheel every time a fourth-grade classroom needs to learn fractions, for example, Bridge standardizes lessons to be used around the world. Instead of aiming to put a tablet in the hands of every student, Bridge puts one in the hands of every teacher, using it to improve teacher attendance and quality of delivery. Instead of trying to make administrative tasks in each school more efficient, Bridge pools all of them together and operates the core systems at headquarters. At every step, Bridge defies assumptions about how a school should be run.

COSTOVATION TRAIT #2: Relentless Focus. To deliver on its mission of providing high-quality education to underserved families, Bridge's founders concentrated on developing a new business model that would dramatically reduce the costs of schooling. This meant centralizing administrative functions, standardizing curriculum, and choosing inexpensive building materials in the construction of their schools.

COSTOVATION TRAIT #3: Blurring Innovation Boundaries. Bridge revolutionizes not what was being taught, but how it was being taught; and in doing so, it completely reconceived school operations. It also utilizes a new way to collect tuition payments—instead of relying on cash or checks, which can be stolen, Bridge allows parents to send money via their mobile phones. This organization is a phenomenal example of looking beyond product innovation to innovate across the business, and it created an entirely new business model in the process.

Innovation isn't just for scientists or the few people with "innovation" in their titles; in fact, it's a mandate that can permeate the organization. Businesses that confine themselves to product innovation miss out on financially rewarding ways to rethink behind-the-scenes processes—and they pass up an opportunity to innovate in their competitors' blind spots.

It's now time to move on to concrete costovation strategies that you and your organization can try on for fit. We'll look at twenty of them in the next section, showing you how others pulled it off, and how you can do the same.

CHAPTER SUMMARY

Product-oriented innovation is common, but it's only the tip of the iceberg for innovation possibilities. Pay attention to operational innovation, which is both incredibly impactful on your bottom line and protective against copycats.

These are the five areas where costovation opportunities are particularly rich, and we recommend considering each of them equally:

1. The **product or service** you are offering
2. How your offering is **made** (e.g., new ways to manufacture and source)
3. How your offering is **delivered** (e.g., new approaches to distribution, transportation, warehousing)
4. How your offering is **sold** (e.g., new interpretations of sales strategies and pricing models)
5. Partnerships with other players within your **ecosystem** (e.g., finding ways to strengthen your value chain, with the ultimate result of strengthening your own business)

A small number of exceptional companies find ways to execute multiple innovations simultaneously across the business. This is more difficult to pull off, but the resulting impact and differentiation can be game changing.

/ part three /

costovation strategy
playbook

Playbook: 20 Costovation Strategies

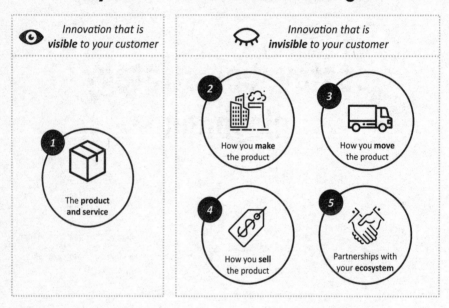

Innovation that is visible to your customer

1 — The **product and service**

Innovation that is invisible to your customer

2 — How you **make** the product

3 — How you **move** the product

4 — How you **sell** the product

5 — Partnerships with your **ecosystem**

chapter 5

•

Twenty Strategies and Tactics

Welcome to the costovation playbook. This is your guide to putting the ideas in this book into action. We'll look at twenty different costovation strategies, showing how they have been used in different contexts and giving practical tips for getting started. Whether you're looking for a better way to grow your business, cut costs, or prepare for anticipated downturns, there's a strategy here for you.

You don't have to read this section in any particular order. Pick an entry that interests you and dive right in.

The **product**
and service

The Product and Service

We'll begin this playbook where most people innovate first: the offering itself. This is the most visible part of your business, whether or not your offering is a tangible item that can be bought on a shelf or shipped in the mail. This section outlines four costovation strategies that we have seen others use to create offerings that zoom in on what matters most—and do far more with less.

1. Simplify the product. Focus on just the features that matter.

Chile is in many ways a model for South America: it boasts the highest per-capita income on the continent and is the only South American member of the OECD, a club of mainly rich countries. And yet, in rural parts of the country, affordable food can be difficult to come by. Supermarkets can be few and far between, and small local shops significantly mark up their goods. Without the option of buying in bulk, many poor Chileans have no choice but to pay up to 40% more for smaller packages.

In 2011, when the country's poverty rate stood at 22.2%, Chilean student Jose Manuel Moller and three friends moved to the outskirts of Santiago, where they saw the lack of budget-friendly food with their own eyes.[1] This inspired them to launch **Algramo**, a company that runs special bulk vending machines full of basic food staples like rice, beans, sugar, and lentils. Customers purchase these staples by the gram (hence the name "Algramo"), using reusable packaging.

Algramo runs an incredibly simple low-cost model, but one that targets unmet customer needs. Since selection is limited to just a handful of everyday, non-perishable food products, prices can be 30–40% lower than what you would find in a traditional supermarket. This also means that Algramo has fewer hassles associated with expired inventory or over-ordering. To secure real estate and win the support of local small businesses, Algramo installs the vending machines for free at local almacenes (similar to bodegas, or compact local stores) and splits margins 50/50 with shopkeepers. Today, Algramo has installed over 475 vending machines and has expanded internationally to Colombia.

The natural progression for any business is to add, add, add. Like dust in a house, feature creep affects all businesses, all the time. But there is great costovation opportunity in simplifying your products and services to what matters most to your customer and subtracting what they are willing to make calculated trade-offs for. For Algramo, this meant stripping out marketing, fancy packaging, and selection in order to make basic food products affordable for over 55,000 people in impoverished areas in South America.

Costovation through product simplification can take many forms. Fast-fashion retailer **Primark**—one of the fastest-growing companies in the U.K.—enabled costovation by selling only private-label products, relying heavily on a handful of synthetic materials and curtailing product reordering. When you look around a Primark store, you'll notice that there are a relatively small number of fabrics being used in any given collection. They've just been cut into a dizzying array of shapes and styles, giving the impression of selection without the complexity. And when an item is gone, it really is gone. This allows Primark to offer a jaw-dropping average price of £4 per item of clothing and enables each store to completely sell through its inventory in just 6 weeks (for comparison, the industry benchmark in 2011 was over 3 months).[2]

Primark concentrates on speed and cost management. What sets Primark apart is that those two attributes—speed and cost—are what matter most to its target customer. Because they deliver so well in those areas, customers are willing to make trade-offs elsewhere, such as on selection, material, and online access.

Costovation Traits: Primark		
Breakthrough Perspective	*Relentless Focus*	*Blurred Innovation Boundaries*
Instead of fearing being out-of-stock, Primark embraces it and makes it part of its central model. When it's gone, it's gone.	Primark focuses narrowly on bringing inexpensively priced clothing to market as fast as possible, and makes tradeoffs in other areas to make that possible.	While Primark's clothes may be trendy, its real innovation comes from a simple business model that creates the impression of selection from a focused number of materials.

WHEN TO USE IT: As a strategy for launching new product lines, this tactic is especially relevant in industries where the competition is pushing upmarket, trying to offer more and more exhaustively complete offerings for premium-paying customers. In those situations, costovation can be a tool for disruptive innovation. Home in on the customer segments that would be satisfied with a simpler, better-targeted offering. These segments are often overlooked.

This strategy can also shine when it comes to expansion in emerging markets. **Embrace**, which produces low-cost infant warmers for premature babies, found a natural home in 22 developing countries. Since Embrace warmers cost 99% less than traditional baby incubators, families in rural areas are able to take a warmer home with their newborn, instead of spending weeks at an expensive hospital.

BEST PRACTICES:

- All businesses can benefit from continually reexamining their offerings and reassessing whether or not they stay true to their intended purpose. We recommend that companies do this regularly to ward off feature creep.
- Remember that costovation is not just about stripping offerings down for the sake of cutting costs. A key part of this kind of innovation is creating something *new* for the customer. It is easier to stay true to that if you commit to being customer-centric. Constantly ask yourself how the changes you propose will deliver new value for your customers.

➡️

TRY THIS:

- Make a list of the attributes that you see are important to your business and offering. Be as expansive as possible. Then identify from this list a small number of items that you consider the strategic core of your offering. What, if subtracted, would make your business no longer a solution to a customer's problem? Finally, examine the rest of your list (the "nice to have's") and question each. Be prepared to let some go.

- Choose a target customer, and list out his or her goals, maybe fifteen or twenty in all. Circle the top five that matter the most to your customer. Now throw the rest out, and think about how your offerings can be improved to excel on each of those top goals—and nothing more.

2. **Use technology to unlock new costovations.** Harness new technology to excel in totally new ways—and at lower costs.

Self-driving cars have captured the imaginations of investors and dominated news outlets around the world. But somewhere off the coast of California, self-driving boats are already a reality.

The **Saildrone** is a sleek vessel, a tall metal sail perched on what looks like a fancy surfboard. It can operate unmanned on the ocean for weeks at a time. It wasn't designed for transportation; rather, these self-driving boats exist primarily to collect data. As they circle the world, they measure things like the temperature of the ocean, the number of fish in an area, the salinity off the coast of a melting iceberg, and the landscape of the ocean floor. Using satellites, that data is beamed thousands of miles away to research scientists working at the National Oceanic and Atmospheric Administration (NOAA).

Before the Saildrone, scientists collected data slowly and painstakingly. They could raise funds for a full-fledged expedition on a traditional scientific research vessel, but that clocked in at a rate of $80,000 a day. They could launch stationary buoys into the water, but then they had to go back to sea to adjust and retrieve them. In comparison, the daily rate for the autonomous Saildrone is just $2,500.[3]

Recent technological advances—coupled with ingenuity—have made the Saildrone possible: the carbon fiber sail that acts like an aircraft wing, the satellite technology that transfers information back to home base, as well as the autopilot programming that navigates via GPS and handles the controls. And with this technology-enabled costovation, not only are scientists able to collect ocean data for pennies on the dollar, but their customer needs are also better satisfied than ever. Now scientists can send out autonomous boats on trips on shorter notice and quickly alter collection patterns in response to changing ocean conditions and interesting discoveries. In time, a fleet of robot sensors placed throughout the ocean could give extensive real-time information about weather phenomena and climate change, and perhaps be used to predict the weather, aid operations of oil and gas companies, and even monitor for illegal fishing.

Costovation Traits: Saildrone		
Breakthrough Perspective	*Relentless Focus*	*Blurred Innovation Boundaries*
Self-driving technology can also be applied to the high seas—and it doesn't have to be used for transportation purposes.	Saildrones are focused on accuracy of data collection, rather than speed or the ability to transport people or objects.	Saildrone combines technological advancements into a new product that comes in at a price point that is just 3% of the cost of a traditional scientific expedition.

Like the Saildrone, there are an increasing number of costovations across industries that are being made possible through technological advancement. **Khan Academy** famously democratized education by disseminating tutorials through YouTube, allowing anyone to learn almost anything, whenever they wanted, for free. In 2017, **MIT researchers** developed prototypes for a pasta that comes out of the box flat like coins, but then twists and curls into rotini and saddle shapes when exposed to water—a technological advancement that could enable companies to make tiny boxes of compact noodles, significantly cutting down on the cost of selling and shipping pasta.[4]

WHEN TO USE IT: Technology is enabling costovation at an increasing pace, and we are seeing it across all industries and business-model types. Keep an open mind about how you—or a savvy competitor—could change the industry with breakthrough technologies.

BEST PRACTICES:

- Stay mindful of breakthrough technologies that can enable costovation where it was unlikely before (e.g., in the case of the shape-shifting MIT pasta), as well as new applications of familiar technologies across industries (e.g., bringing YouTube to education, as Sal Khan did).

■ Remember that the costovation strategies in this playbook are not mutually exclusive. Consider how technological advances can couple with other tactics to bring to market a truly unprecedented offering.

TRY THIS:

- As you monitor the latest technological advancements— whether breakthrough or incremental—explore what potential uses they may have for both lowering costs and increasing customer delight. What could they allow you to do much better, even if it would require doing other things worse, and what customer segment would joyfully accept those trade-offs?

- Examine technological innovations in industries outside your own. Are there ways to reapply those discoveries in a way that no one in your field has done before?

3. **Dissolve the wall between operations and customer experience.** Let customers participate.

■

In 1997, **Build-A-Bear Workshop** introduced a daring new business model to the toy industry: customers would pay large sums—perhaps $60 apiece—for the privilege of providing the free labor to make their own stuffed animal.

At the beginning, founder Maxine Clark encountered only confused mall landlords. You want to rent out mall space to have kids make a mess with synthetic stuffing? But it didn't take long before the concept took off like a rocket. Lines went out the door, malls were begging for Build-A-Bear Workshops to lease space, and the company started to turn away investors after just a few years. Kids loved that they could customize how their stuffed animal looked and sounded, that they used their own feet to pump out the stuffing, and that they could ceremoniously grant life to their creation by inserting a cloth heart. The once-sealed-off operation of stuffing teddy bears became the core attraction of this store.

Build-A-Bear's key insight was that the toy experience didn't have to be limited to just the joy of the object itself: rather, the making of the toy could be a unique bonding experience between parent and child, or limitless entertainment at a birthday party. As Maxine Clark put it, "I believe that we don't sell products. We sell smiles."[5]

Operations are often the hidden back end of businesses, but Build-A-Bear Workshop shows how shining a spotlight on operations can excite customers in new ways—while also streamlining its supply chain, reducing the bulky items needing transportation, and carving out a niche that could withstand fickle toy trends. We have also seen this strategy in the restaurant industry: for instance, consider Chinese "hot pot" restaurants, which provide chopped meats and vegetables for diners to cook to their tastes at their table.

WHEN TO USE IT: Use this strategy to differentiate yourself in tightly competitive, seemingly commoditized industries where customers still care about the product they are purchasing. This tactic is a phenomenal way to address emotional jobs to be done (like sharing an experience or spending time with a

Costovation Traits: Build-A-Bear Workshop		
ᴏᴏ	⇩ ⇨○⇦ ⇧	🏃 L
Breakthrough Perspective	*Relentless Focus*	*Blurred Innovation Boundaries*
Building the toy can be as much of a joy as the toy itself.	Build-A-Bear focuses on building a memorable customer experience for children. This means bringing children along for everything from stuffing the bear to watching a staff member stitch the bear closed. Build-A-Bear resisted the temptation to move these parts of the process backstage.	Build-A-Bear Workshop makes the operations of creating a stuffed animal the core attraction. The bonding with the bear starts not with its receipt, but at its creation.

loved one). By doing so, you can help yourself stand out from others in profound ways.

BEST PRACTICES:

- To create a customer experience that really sticks, you need to have a strong understanding of what the customer wants. Customers may have a hard time articulating this (what focus group would have said that they would be willing to wait around an extra five minutes so that someone could sew up their bear?), so we advocate passive observation as well as triangulating questions that approach a topic from multiple angles.
- Sometimes we unwittingly create new pain points even as we successfully solve unmet needs. It's important to carefully consider the implications of bringing your operations fully to the customer. We don't recommend this approach for the sausage-making industry!

➡️ **TRY THIS:**

- Imagine that your customers want to take a bigger role in the creation of your final product. What stages or elements of the production process can your customers feasibly participate in? For the areas where you don't think customers should participate, ask yourself why, and examine if you are subscribing to traditional assumptions.

- Once you have an idea of how you might redesign the customer experience, draw out a journey map showing how your customers would interact with this new concept. You may need multiple journey maps to cover distinct contexts. At each step in the map, be sure to think about what new pain points may arise and how you can address them.

4. Build a platform. Create the foundation for growth.

■

There are few kitchen tools that have the allure and staying power that the **KitchenAid** Stand Mixer does. Generations of people have saved up for one of these brightly painted kitchen status symbols, which sell for up to $500 each. The wedding website The Knot writes that the KitchenAid Stand Mixer is "by-far the single most registered-for item" by brides-to be, and even for people who don't cook, the mixer is an announcement to the world that "I'm a serious cook" or, at the very least, "I got married."[6]

The core of the stand mixer is a stainless-steel bowl and a 325-watt motor. But the attachment options are endless: you can use it to mix cake batter, mash potatoes, knead dough, beat eggs, cut fresh pasta, churn ice cream, mill grains, mince garlic, *and* shred cheese. The KitchenAid is based on a foundational platform product that has not changed in decades; if you find old attachments from the 1950s, they'll still work in your modern KitchenAid. This means that the innovation focus can shift from the platform to the attachments. And, brilliantly, it is through the attachments that the company has the ultimate flexibility to adapt to changing customer preferences. Seventy years ago, people wanted to use their KitchenAids to shell peas, buff silver, and open cans. In this modern day, KitchenAid stays trendy simply by issuing new attachments for spiralizing zucchini and juicing fruit.

Costovation Traits: KitchenAid		
Breakthrough Perspective	*Relentless Focus*	*Blurred Innovation Boundaries*
The mixer motor doesn't need to change every few years to keep up with consumer trends. Instead, KitchenAid innovates on the attachments.	KitchenAid focuses on creating a kitchen tool that can be infinitely multi-purpose—without chasing all those features at once.	KitchenAid's platform model is an operational innovation that helps reduce the cost of bringing new features to market.

The **John Deere** tractor is another great example of the platform model: the tractor is a foundation for innumerable attachments like plows, mowers, and cutters of all varieties.

Over the last two decades, the business of creating platforms has exploded in popularity and has been enabled by new technologies to include outside participants. **Apple's** App Store ecosystem, for instance, allows outside developers to create new uses and new value for the iPhone and iPad that are beyond Apple's imagination. These apps—like Snapchat, Uber, and Instagram—helped cement the iPhone's importance in our day-to-day lives. **Facebook's** developer ecosystem similarly brings in third-party companies to build features and attractions that keep users on its site for longer. These two tech giants built solid foundations for their businesses, and then handed off the baton to others to participate in, contribute to, and share in their business growth.

Here are a few other platforms that have scaled exponentially:

- **Yelp** runs a platform where the true value of the site—reviews on restaurants and shops—is created by unpaid users.
- **Wikipedia's** free online encyclopedia platform transfers the editorial work to its readers, who willingly take on the thankless burden of editing and building articles.
- **YouTube** was the first video-hosting platform to go mainstream. Instead of having to curate videos, YouTube passed on the creative production to its users.

WHEN TO USE IT: Platform businesses are built to scale quickly, making them a top option for aggressive growth. They are also used as a source of competitive advantage and differentiation. Pay special attention to ensure that your platform is attractive to partners, and that others haven't beaten you to the punch by being the first to scale up a platform for the target job to be done.

BEST PRACTICES:

- Platform growth can be a strictly internal activity (e.g., KitchenAid and John Deere creating new attachments for their core offerings), or it can involve outsiders (e.g., Apple and Facebook running developer ecosystems). Weigh the pros and cons of both for your context.

- Platform businesses involving third parties are far from being hands-off businesses. Apple, for example, sets rigorous guidelines and expectations for participants on its App Store. Plan ahead for how you'll manage the community, keep them engaged, and maintain quality. Platform businesses have the virtue of being able to scale expeditiously, but their deaths can also be speedy.

- If you will depend on outside parties to add value to your platform, think carefully about how you will create the initial momentum. We recommend starting with a focused customer set, whose needs and jobs to be done you can home in on. Deliver there and provide proof of concept before expanding. Prepare to participate on your own platform to stimulate activity and model the intended behavior; when **Quora** first started, editors would ask the questions and then answer the questions themselves.

TRY THIS:

- Platforms involving outside parties are often centered around the idea of exchange. Carefully articulate the core interaction for your platform ideas. What do both your participants and your company get out of the platform? Make sure you are also clear about who the *producer* of value and the *consumer* of value are for your platform ideas.

- Brainstorm different ways you can monetize your platform (e.g., transaction fee, pay for access, pay for premium content).

How you **make**
the product

How You Make the Product

Many of the most-lauded innovations in the world are innovations we can touch and see, like a new smartphone or a self-driving car. But plenty of innovations also happen behind the scenes, resulting in processes that are faster and less costly—and harder to copy. In this section, we dive into six costovation strategies related to manufacturing and the act of *making*.

5. **Handle the network, not the goods.** Create an asset-light operation by focusing on services or on facilitating a network of transactions.

■

Asking someone to marry you might rank as one of the most nerve-racking experiences in a person's life—and the engagement-ring industry isn't known for helping to alleviate those anxieties. Engagement-ring pricing is notoriously opaque and fickle; you won't know how much that sparkly solitaire will cost you until you visit a jewelry store and ask. On top of that, purchasers are often first-time fine-jewelry buyers, and salespeople ham up the fact that you'll (hopefully) only ever make this kind of purchase once.

Facing off against these clear pain points, online shopping for engagement rings has become increasingly popular in recent years. Shoppers like the fact that they can browse a seemingly limitless selection, at their own pace, in the privacy of their home. And then there is the discounting: rings bought online are often 30 to 50% off those bought in brick-and-mortar stores.

How do online retailers manage to pull off such steep discounts? For **JamesAllen.com**, the secret is that there is no grand diamond vault. That's right; they don't physically own the diamonds that they feature on their website. Instead, they run a modified drop-ship model. Once an order is placed, the diamond is sent from the manufacturer to James Allen for inspection, before then being sent on to the customer. This means that instead of employing salespeople, maintaining an extensive showroom, and paying up-front for inventory, James Allen can focus on being more or less a technology company: it can pour its resources into running a website, perfecting its diamond photography, and keeping a small number of staff around for customer service and diamond inspection. In addition to being able to offer among the lowest prices in the industry, they are also able to respond faster to new market conditions and trends.

Costovation Traits: James Allen		
⬯⬯ *Breakthrough Perspective*	⬇ ⇨◇⇦ ⬆ *Relentless Focus*	🏃 *Blurred Innovation Boundaries*
The costs for inventory and sales in a traditional brick-and-mortar jewelry store can be enormous. James Allen tackles both.	James Allen's singular focus is on engagement rings, rather than other types of jewelry.	James Allen's modified drop-ship model is behind-the-scenes and invisible to the customer—except, of course, in the price.

We see this costovation tactic—of managing a network rather than the goods—in many industries. **Drizly**, an online order service for on-demand alcohol delivery, navigates the legal complexities of the three-tier system of alcohol distribution in the U.S. without owning (or even touching!) any liquor. Instead, it manages a marketplace that connects liquor retailers with individual customers. When a customer places an order on the Drizly app, Drizly alerts a local partner liquor retailer, which fulfills and delivers the order. Customers don't pay an extra delivery fee; instead, that cost is shouldered by the retail partners, who pay for a monthly license. In this way, Drizly never touches a bottle of alcohol or a cent from the transaction. Meanwhile, **Xometry** matches businesses looking for a manufacturer with industrial factories having excess capacity and adds extra value by streamlining the bidding process and offering instant pricing and partner-matching.

WHEN TO USE IT: The most revolutionary applications of this strategy occur in industries that are traditionally asset-heavy, such as jewelry, beverages, and industrial manufacturing. But that's not always the case: **TaskRabbit** connects temporary part-time workers with people looking for help with odd tasks, like assembling Ikea furniture, calling event guests to ask for RSVPs, or weeding the garden. TaskRabbit gives much-needed visibility to people looking for work, and it helps others cross items off their to-do list in a timely and cost-effective way.

BEST PRACTICES:

- Network-based business models can be used to different ends: to lower prices (James Allen), to increase access and visibility (TaskRabbit), or even to create a new offering

(Drizly). Be clear about what goal your network aims to achieve.

■ Think about and defend the incentive your suppliers have to participate in your network. TaskRabbit tapped into a population of temporary workers eager to get their names out in front of potential jobs. Drizly helps liquor retailers connect with their customers in new ways. James Allen brings visibility to diamond wholesalers who previously had no other way to connect with their end customers.

TRY THIS:

- As you imagine your network and develop the details around it, map out the value proposition that your network would bring for three key stakeholder types—you, your participating suppliers, and your customers. What does this network help do that couldn't easily be done otherwise? What functional and emotional jobs are you helping these stakeholders get done? What would incentivize participation?

6. **Costovate through external innovation.** Use external innovation to lower the costs—and the risks—around new product development.

■

Innovation is often mistaken for its close cousin research & development. That association leads to the misunderstanding that innovation is always expensive in time and resources, and that innovation is always an internal process. Not so.

External innovation—also called open innovation in some circles—is the concept of companies working together toward creating something new. For example, many technology and pharmaceutical companies partner with universities to stay up to date on the latest research; this is cheaper and faster than funding that research in-house. For large companies, bringing in outside innovation partners can cut development timelines in half.

Colgate-Palmolive is a super-user of external innovation; in fact, the company views itself as a formulator of externally supplied technologies. Colgate-Palmolive works with a number of suppliers that it "steers" toward its particular needs. The consumer-goods giant helps its partners secure funding (e.g., by vouching for them to a grant agency, or identifying possible sources of funding), but the ultimate responsibility for development falls to the suppliers. A notable example of Colgate-Palmolive's external innovation successes is the Colgate Wisp, a compact, disposable, single-use toothbrush that won the 2010 "Product of the Year" award from Fast Company.[7] To bring this product to life, Colgate collaborated closely with Trisa, a Swiss manufacturer—just as it has done with countless other researchers, academics, and suppliers to launch nearly 800 products per year.

Costovation Traits: Colgate-Palmolive		
ᴼᴼ *Breakthrough Perspective*	⇩ ⇨○⇦ ⇧ *Relentless Focus*	🏃 *Blurred Innovation Boundaries*
Colgate-Palmolive realized that it didn't have to go after innovation alone.	Colgate-Palmolive focuses on a narrow number of suppliers with whom it invests resources and time into developing a relationship of trust.	The results of external innovation at Colgate-Palmolive are not limited to just what customers can see when they buy Colgate-Palmolive products—changes can also be "behind the scenes" (e.g., manufacturing).

There are many different models for external innovation. Whereas Colgate-Palmolive works closely with its suppliers, others such as **Netflix** and **Starbucks** utilize more of a collective approach. In 2013, for instance, Netflix held an innovation competition to find ways to improve the usability and quality of its cloud-streaming platform; there were ten prizes of $10,000 each. Starbucks runs a website called My Starbucks Idea, in which customers submit ideas and vote for ones they like best. You can thank clever Starbucks fans for ideas like the splash sticks that prevent coffee from escaping to-go cup lids.

WHEN TO USE IT: External innovation can take many shapes and forms, ranging from quicker and lighter-touch (like a one-off idea competition) to complex and long term (like equity investments). As a result, it has many applications. That said, a word to the wise: we often see that the overall culture of innovation at the company can disproportionately affect the success of external innovation initiatives. The "not invented here" syndrome is common and can be toxic.

BEST PRACTICES:

■ External innovation can be applied to all parts of a business; it can be used to generate new recipes just as much as it can be used to create new forms of packaging and other process design elements. Consider it in its broadest form.

■ There are many models for external innovation. In addition to the supplier-led innovation model at Colgate-Palmolive, the innovation competition at Netflix, and the idea-collection network at Starbucks, external innovation may also look like joint ventures and equity investments, among other options.

■ External innovation is not a silver bullet. It requires a sub-stantial amount of oversight and planning to ensure that the results can be implemented by the host organization. A tale of caution: Netflix's first innovation competition, held in 2006, awarded an eye-popping $1 million prize for a film-predicting algorithm that it eventually realized it could not actually use.

TRY THIS:

• Research the different models of external innovation that have been used in your industry as well as others. Explore how you might apply them to your context.

• Assess the culture of innovation at your firm. Are you ready for outside partners to weigh in on your innovation efforts? Is there an internal champion who can ensure the success of an external innovation initiative?

7. **Save the customization for later.** Deploy postponement techniques to make personalization and customization more efficient.

■

Postponement involves delaying customization until farther down the supply chain. An instant ramen maker, for instance, can create just one ramen product—and then slip powdered flavor packets into each package to create dozens of different ramen varieties. Postponement can reduce the number of unique items that you manage, as well as cut down on distri-bution costs, while enabling you to respond faster to unique demands. Customers also relish in being able to modify and tailor the product to their liking.

For example:

- **Reebok** stores plain jerseys in a distribution center in Indianapolis, where they are screen-printed and embroidered according to demand, such as for players who demonstrated recent heroics.
- The **Mini** earned fame as a car of nearly infinite customization—made possible because nearly all of the customization options are surface-level details that are highly visible to the consumer but have almost no impact on the supply chain. In fact, some customization details are applied as late in the process as at the dealer.
- Packets of **Salt'n'Shake**, one of the U.K.'s most beloved potato chip brands, come with a blue sachet containing salt, allowing the purchaser to salt the chips to his or her taste—and freeing the company from having to produce no-salt, lightly salted, and regularly salted varieties.
- **Comex**, the largest paint producer, distributor, and retailer in Mexico, stocks its stores with just white paint, along with the chemicals needed to turn white paint into thousands of other colors. Once a customer places an order, store employees mix together the requested colors immediately.

Costovation Traits: Salt'n'Shake		
ᗝᗜ	⇩⇨○⇦⇧	🏃
Breakthrough Perspective	*Relentless Focus*	*Blurred Innovation Boundaries*
It's not inconveniencing a customer to have them season their own food to their liking; in fact, they may prefer it.	Salt'n'Shake zoomed in on its manufacturing process, seeking ways to reduce the number of items that it produced.	Salt'n'Shake's approach to seasoning was both a boon for its marketers (who could advertise it as a chip for everyone) as well as its operations specialists (who reaped the benefits of having reduced SKUs).

WHEN TO USE IT: Postponement is relevant to any company dealing with a rapidly rising number of stock keeping units (SKUs) or products with small variations. Delivering on those demands for customization often means complicating the supply chain: the number of SKUs increases, lines have to be cleared and reset, inventory increases, and there's greater uncertainty for forecasting.

BEST PRACTICES:

- Keep a wide definition of *where* postponement can occur (e.g., at the distribution center, at the warehouse, at the point of sale, at the point of consumption), as well as *what* is postponed (e.g., labeling, packaging, assembly).
- Be prepared: postponement usually involves some cross-departmental teamwork. R&D can be a critical ally in devising new formulations of the product. Finance needs to be consulted if there is capital expenditure to change production-line configurations. Quality assurance and compliance teams can point out quality or regulatory implications that you might not have thought of. Engage these stakeholders early and often.

TRY THIS:

- Identify where customization or product differentiation occurs in your current supply chain today. This is your starting point. From here, explore how you can delay customization. Brainstorm postponement possibilities for different aspects of your product (e.g., packaging, flavoring), as well as at the following points in the supply chain: at the distribution center, at the warehouse, at the point of sale, and at the point of consumption. For each postponement opportunity, be realistic about the trade-offs that may be required (e.g., quality control, losing out on economies of scale), as well as unintended consequences.

8. **Speed up build time with modularization.** Accelerate the time it takes to build by breaking the product into smaller chunks.

■

The tiny European **Smart Car** is known for its fuel economy and affordability—a thriftiness that extends all the way through the way the car is manufactured. In a traditional auto factory, the supplier drops off a shipment of auto parts—tires, steering wheels, engine parts—and drives away. At the Smart Car factory in northeastern France, however, the suppliers bring partially assembled car parts and install them onto the final cars using their own employees. The company calls this a modular assembly system.

For MCC, the parent company of the Smart Car, this is a fantastic arrangement. They are relieved of the financial and legal liabilities for its supplier-installed parts. Their HR footprint is reduced, since the majority of the factory workers (1,100 of the total 1,800) are managed by the suppliers. They don't need as much financial overhead to fund the product, since development costs are shared with the suppliers. And modular assembly saves time: it takes just 4.5 hours to assemble each car.[8] If this system sounds familiar, you aren't mistaken; Smart Car was conceived by the same people, using the same type of manufacturing strategies and personalization features, who popularized the Swatch watch brand.

Costovation Traits: Smart Car		
⊙⊙ *Breakthrough Perspective*	⇨○⇦ *Relentless Focus*	🏃 *Blurred Innovation Boundaries*
Smart Car doesn't have to build the whole car by itself.	Smart Car focused on making its assembly line as fast and lightweight as possible. The car itself is fairly basic.	While the world ogled at its car's low prices and compact sizing, Smart Car's greatest innovation was behind the scenes in its modular construction.

Modular building is not just for manufacturers, however. In education, **Western Governor's University** has dramatically lowered tuition by hiring separate sets of staff: specialist faculty to develop courses, teaching faculty to provide instruction, assessment faculty for testing, and advisement faculty for student support. **Taco Bell** shrank its kitchens and eliminated stovetops by outsourcing the cooking of its meat to its suppliers (this also decreases the amount of time it takes to assemble a Taco Bell meal; staff just need to reheat the meat and assemble). And **CitizenM**, a boutique chain of affordable luxury hotels, built a new 300-room hotel in New York City in 2017 using a set of 210 pods shipped from Poland. When the pods arrived in New York, they were simply installed into a skeleton structure, bypassing many of the risky building processes that usually take place many stories in the air. Project officials said that the choice to use the modular construction method reduced the completion schedule by two to five months and has resulted in 1,200 fewer trips that trucks must make on their way to the job site. Modular building has also helped CitizenM monitor quality and consistency, since prefabrication factories offer a controlled environment.

WHEN TO USE IT: Modularization may be a good fit for companies that are particularly focused on shortening the time it takes to build or assemble, and on reducing overhead. The drawback can be constraints imposed on customization.

BEST PRACTICES:

■ Modularization isn't a "go-it-alone" approach. Smart Car relied heavily upon its network of suppliers to take on the task of car assembly; CitizenM depended upon a clever builder in Poland. Take a good look at your suppliers' willingness and ability to make modularization a reality.

■ The trade-off with modularization is that too much standardization can impact flexibility. Be clear up front about what your strategic priorities are and the trade-offs you are willing to make, then reassess whether modularization makes sense for you.

TRY THIS:

- As a rule, flexibility and customization matter to all businesses, regardless of industry. But there is variation in the degree to which it matters—and where. Identify areas for your offering or business where standardization is passable, or even welcome. That will form the starting point for exploring modularization options.

- Work together with suppliers, or even your sales-channel partners, to explore how they might be able to support modularization. They may be delighted to become an even more integral partner.

9. Find intention in waste. Reduce waste—or find new uses for it.

■

The **California Cedar Products Company**, Cal Cedar for short, is a family-owned company that has been producing pencils in the U.S. for over a hundred years. Starting in the 1960s, Cal Cedar started eyeing expansion opportunities—what else could it do given its assets and expertise in cedar?

Cal Cedar's approach was remarkably down-to-earth. Instead of investing heavily in speculative technologies, it experimented with what it had: an abundance of unwanted cedar shavings and sawdust. After mixing bits of wood with various wax blends, Cal Cedar invented the world's first manufactured firelog, the DuraFlame. Customers loved that these new logs were easy to light and burned cleanly and attractively. Today, that product generates over $250 million in annual revenue.

The brilliance of the DuraFlame was that it combined two industrial byproducts—sawdust and petroleum wax—to create a new product that exceeded its traditional log competitors on multiple fronts, while also satisfying pain points for sawmills. Sawmills were more than eager to part with their ever-growing piles of wood scraps; in fact, they often paid others to haul away their sawdust. In Cal Cedar's new business model, the company was being paid to receive its primary raw material.

Costovation Traits: California Cedar Products Company		
ᴏᴏ	⇩ ⇨○⇦ ⇧	🏃
Breakthrough Perspective	*Relentless Focus*	*Blurred Innovation Boundaries*
One man's trash (in this case, sawdust) is another man's treasure (or a quarter of a billion dollar business).	The DuraFlame doesn't claim to be good for heating or cooking; it's just a reliably good-looking firelog. Cal Cedar picked its battles.	Cal Cedar created a business model in which it was paid to accept its primary raw material.

We've seen this costovation strategy in the food industry as well. **Nestlé's** clever use for imperfect Kit Kat bars was to crush them up and repurpose them as filling for other Kit Kats. And **Intermarché**, a French supermarket chain, started selling "ugly" produce with cosmetic blemishes at a 30% discount in 2014—cutting down on food waste and winning the hearts of sustainability-minded customers (in fact, store traffic increased 24% during the first month of Intermarché's "Inglorious Fruits and Vegetables" campaign).

WHEN TO USE IT: Most applications of this strategy involve companies with physical offerings, such as pencils, fruit, and candy bars.

BEST PRACTICES:

- Cal Cedar used byproducts to create an entirely new product line, but don't forget to consider how the same thinking can be used to improve existing products (like Nestlé did with its Kit Kats).
- Consider how this tactic can be paired with others to craft a broader solution that solves unmet needs while still cutting costs.

TRY THIS:

- Brainstorm a list of the "waste" that your industry produces. Map out what currently happens to that waste and identify the pain points throughout that process. Thinking broadly about this list, consider how waste can be put to new uses— the makings of a new product, being recycled back into the final product, or other ways to impact product positioning or operations. What value can we add to waste?

10. **Put people where they matter.** Embrace new approaches to human resourcing.

■

There is a nondescript room somewhere in Cleveland where, every night from 7 p.m. to 7 a.m., a handful of doctors and nurses diligently keep watch over 200 patients in intensive care units. But this is no ordinary hospital, and there are no actual patients in the bunker. In fact, the patients may be hundreds or even thousands of miles away. Instead, the focal point of this room is a wall of beeping screens representing live data—vitals, labs, agitation, video footage, even pupil dilation.

This medical command center—dubbed the eHospital—is an innovation brainchild from the world-famous **Cleveland Clinic**. From this room, a small number of doctors can focus on monitoring vitals and crunching data. If any patients encounter issues, these doctors can send an alert to a nurse on the ground. Patients benefit from a more comfortable experience; instead of being awoken at odd hours of the night as nurses make their rounds, they can rest in privacy. Eventually, the Cleveland Clinic aspires to have patients bring this technology home with them so that they can be monitored from

Costovation Traits: Cleveland Clinic's eHospital		
Breakthrough Perspective	*Relentless Focus*	*Blurred Innovation Boundaries*
Physically monitoring patients is not the only—or even necessarily the best—way of checking on them.	The Cleveland Clinic focused on finding the best way to leverage data and analytics to deliver patient care. A central command center emerged as a solution.	Cleveland Clinic is tinkering with all aspects of healthcare delivery—from the equipment used to monitor patient vitals to the way nurses check in on them.

the comfort of their own bedrooms (and ultimately reduce their length of stay in the hospital).

This costovation technique takes a close look at human resourcing and puts people where they matter most. For the Cleveland Clinic, this means centralizing patient data to be analyzed by a smaller night-shift nursing team. Many companies such as **Southwest Airlines** let their call-center employees work from home, since what matters is the people, not the fact that they are all working together in the same building.

Sometimes it's more than physical location that matters. **MSNBC** broke free of its three-company race with CNN and Fox News by hiring people with a talent for political commentary, rather than traditional reporting experience. This helped the network surge ahead in popularity among its liberal fan base—analysis, not reporting, was what they craved—while also boasting the lowest production costs per viewer. **Acton Academy Network**, a collective of over fifty private schools in the U.S. and abroad, throws out the idea of grade levels ("When have you ever had a workplace where everyone around you was within six months of your age?" asked Chief Evangelist Matt Clayton), and instead empowers a small number of learning guides to push students to do their own learning at their own pace. As a result of this different approach to staffing, the network is able to operate at a cost of roughly $4,000 a student per year.[9] Compare that to the $10,651 that state and federal governments spend to send a kid to public school for one year.[10]

WHEN TO USE IT: This costovation technique can be helpful where there is a dearth of talent, such as a shortage of physicians or experienced broadcast journalists. It can also be used to increase employee satisfaction or help with recruiting (e.g., by redefining a job position).

BEST PRACTICES:

- Identify what matters to your people, and focus on that. Acton Academy understood that many teachers are frustrated by administrative burdens and other tedious items that keep them from feeling like teachers, so it found a new way to empower them. Southwest Airlines reduced the commute for its call center employees to zero.

TRY THIS:

- Throughout this book, we have advocated for thorough research on your customers, but you can also turn the spotlight on your own employees. What are their jobs to be done? What excites them about their work? What drags them down?

- Imagine you could throw out all job descriptions and reporting lines at your organization and redesign things from scratch, with an eye on customer satisfaction, efficiency, and your overall mission. What would you change? What would you keep the same?

How You Move the Product

Delivery and distribution are yet another area ripe for innovation. In this short section, we identify two costovation strategies that we've seen applied to how companies physically move their products, from origin facility all the way to the customer's hands.

11. **Bypass steps in the value chain.** Vertically integrate and play supply-chain leapfrog.

■

The Internet made it easy for anyone to start their own business from the comfort of their home or some other hidden location; no longer was a brick-and-mortar presence necessary. The Internet also enabled thousands of companies to unwittingly costovate in their value chain. Because they can now send products directly to customers, they can cut out distributors, wholesalers, and other middlemen—ultimately delivering major cost savings for their customers. We've seen this vertically integrated, direct-to-customer business model in countless categories:

- **M.Gemi** sells luxury Italian leather shoes for under $300, sending them straight to customers' doors. It does so by forming partnerships with Italian craftsmen and smaller factories in need of work. To keep its styles fresh, it retires shoe styles after just three months on the site. By the end of 2017, M.Gemi raised $52 million in venture capital.

- **Hubble** ships daily disposable contact lenses to customers for $30 a month, giving consumers a new option in an industry where four lens manufacturers control nearly 95% of the U.S. market and where the average cost for dailies amounts to $700 a year or more. Hubble partners with Taiwanese contact-lens manufacturer St. Shine Optical to make its lenses. Within its first nine months of operation, Hubble reached $20 million in subscriptions. Longer term, Hubble aims to make daily lenses the preferred choice in the U.S. (over "monthlies" and "bi-weeklies"), like they are elsewhere in the world.

- **Everlane** retails "elevated basics" like white t-shirts, cashmere sweaters, and leather tote bags through its website. Everlane is radically transparent about its pricing and for each item breaks down the cost of every component as well as its own margin, which is usually a fraction of what its competitors charge.

- Insurance companies like startup **Lemonade** sell directly to the customer, instead of through brokers who usually take a hefty commission.

Selling directly to consumers brings a number of benefits. In addition to lowering overall costs, this strategy allows companies to control the markdowns on their products, their overall branding and product presentation, and customer data. It grants them freedom from the sometimes-tyrannical rules that traditional channels like department stores may impose (e.g., charging extra fees for advertising, or demanding an unlimited right to return orders). The downside is that it can require significant capital to get started, and customers may not be familiar or immediately comfortable with purchasing an item online that they have not yet seen. And, no matter how amazing your price point, you also have to get your customers' attention in the first place.

Costovation Traits: M.Gemi		
ᗝᗝ	⇨◯⇦	🏃
Breakthrough Perspective	*Relentless Focus*	*Blurred Innovation Boundaries*
There is a win-win to be had in luxury shoes: customers want high-quality goods at low prices, and smaller Italian factories with excess capacity are looking for work.	M.Gemi focuses on providing a great shoe for a low price, and forfeits providing an endless selection. Shoes are produced in limited batches, and when they are gone, they are gone.	M.Gemi's innovation is made possible from synergetic relationships with vendors in their supply chains.

WHEN TO USE IT: Direct-to-customer brands do well in industries that have traditionally enjoyed high profit margins and tightly controlled distribution, like mattresses and prescription eyeglasses. They also can inject personality and fun into categories that have become stale purchases over time.

BEST PRACTICES:

■ Though online shopping is common behavior today in the United States, there are still many people who are resistant to it for certain categories of products. In a 2016 Nielsen Global Connected Commerce survey across 26 countries, for instance, 45% of respondents had never shopped for fashion online.[11] It will be key to assuage any concerns these people may have about purchasing items without seeing them first in person (e.g., fit predictors, easy returns and exchanges).

- Take full advantage of this opportunity to shape your brand's messaging, build a relationship with customers, and collect and use data to better understand your customers.

- One of the most challenging aspects of the direct-to-consumer model is getting your name out there, and in this respect traditional channels tend to take the upper hand. Think carefully about how you will resource your advertising and marketing efforts to cut through the noise. You may be able to eliminate a sales channel but not the functions that it serves.

TRY THIS:

- Think through why your organization or industry currently does not sell directly to the customer. For each reason, stay mindful of the assumptions you may be making and explore ways to subvert them.

- Look through analogous examples of the vertically integrated business model from other industries that share similar characteristics to yours. For example, a tech company might look to fast fashion for examples of innovation in a trend-dominated space.

12. **Zoom in on last-mile delivery.** Pay special attention to the cost-
    liest step in a parcel's journey.

                                    ▪

In 1975, there were only three cities in the world with populations greater than 10 million people: New York, Tokyo,
and Mexico City. By 2030, there are predicted to be 41 (and
only three of them will be in North America). For most of the
earth's population, the future is urban. Are your delivery and
distribution systems ready?

Tokyo—a city that has long been crowned a megacity—
has been forced by necessity to rethink last-mile distribution
systems. Take **Shinjuku Matenro**, which manages office deliveries in a particularly compact area of downtown Tokyo where
130,000 workers can be found in just twenty high-rise buildings. Shinjuku uses a joint delivery system with micro-urban
distribution centers: trucks run loops between distribution
centers and office-building loading docks, and then a separate
team makes individual deliveries within the office buildings by
hand. Tailoring the distribution channel to the unique context of downtown office buildings helps the company make its
deliveries smoother and faster than before.

End customers are usually not aware of the processes and
the journey their parcel has gone through before arriving
at their address, but one thing is certain: they do factor the
speed and accuracy of final delivery into their overall experience. Many companies are investing large sums into rev-
olutionizing last-mile delivery, employing technologies like
drones, robots, driverless vehicles, and advanced algorithms
and analytics. But as Shinjuku Matenro shows, innovating on
last-mile delivery doesn't have to be a high-tech speculative
activity.

Neither does it have to be focused on urban areas. **Hindustan Unilever**, for instance, tailored its distribution channels for rural India. The sixteen-wheelers that Unilever employs to deliver to big box stores in Europe are impractical there; these small, remote villages require a new solution. Unilever's response was a program called Shakti Amma, which empowers local entrepreneurs (often women) to sell Unilever products in their villages, having picked up small quantities from their district salesperson.

Costovation Traits: Hindustan Unilever's Shakti Amma		
Breakthrough Perspective	Relentless Focus	Blurred Innovation Boundaries
Distribution systems should be tailored to their context; the methods that have worked elsewhere in the world don't make sense for rural India.	In this innovative program, Unilever focuses on increasing access to its products.	While many think that Unilever's greatest innovations are in branding and new product creation, the company has a remarkable history of rethinking distribution models.

WHEN TO USE IT: This line of thinking is especially important for companies selling tangible products that need to be physically made, moved, and sold, like office supplies and facial soap. It is applicable in emerging and developed markets, as well as for rural and urban geographies; each of these has its own challenges and unmet needs that demand a fresh new look at distribution.

BEST PRACTICES:

- Market research can be critical here to help understand what customers are looking for in last-mile delivery. You may be able to guess at what they want based on your own experience and the complaints you've heard, but it's important to speak to the customers themselves to ensure that you are designing systems that truly speak to them—and that don't overshoot what they need. We also recommend that you shadow a delivery in the target geography to experience the struggles and challenges firsthand. For instance, when Stephen once hitched a ride on a beverage delivery truck in Africa, he observed that cash was counted seven times between the time it was initially paid and when it was banked. Shadowing will help you understand what it is that you are solving for.

TRY THIS:

- Draw out the distribution journey map for your products. Identify areas of potential weakness, frustration, or inefficiency.

- Compare how companies in other categories who share your target customers are handling last-mile delivery. Are there lessons you can glean and apply to your own context?

- Get out of the office and follow a few deliveries yourself. Take careful notes about pain points that arise, and be mindful of the ways that pain points can shift, depending on the context (e.g., if it is raining, if you are delivering to a rural farmhouse).

How you **sell**
the product

How You Sell the Product

In this section of the *Costovation Playbook*, we study five costovation strategies that have revolutionized the way companies sell their offerings.

13. **Don't underestimate the power of self-service.** Let products sell themselves.

■

Software sales is not a cheap business to be in; incumbents like IBM, Oracle, and Hewlett Packard Enterprise employ thousands of commissioned salespeople to crisscross the world, calling on potential customers and giving training demonstrations. But there is one up-and-coming disruptor that everyone in the enterprise-software industry knows: **Atlassian**, a young Australian firm valued at over $5 billion, that, against all conventional wisdom, has no sales department at all.

Atlassian practices complete transparency. All prices, product information, and documentation are on its website for prospective customers to browse at their own pace. The software itself is designed to be supremely simple to download and install by yourself. Customers train themselves using online training materials.

But the 60,000 companies around the world that use Atlassian products don't mind that the tool is more or less self-service. In fact, Atlassian's key insight was that software developers may actually *prefer* this low-pressure, hands-off approach. These are folks who love digging through the details themselves, and who would do almost anything to avoid a sales call. By nailing this customer preference, Atlassian created a self-sustaining "marketing movement." In fact, Atlassian users are so passionate about the software (and pleased that they are "in the know" about a great new tool) that they are more than willing to do the hard work of spreading the word about Atlassian, for free. Most of the adoption of Atlassian products comes ground-up from rank-and-file software developers, rather than from big enterprise-level contracts signed by company leaders.

Costovation Traits: Atlassian		
ᴖᴖ	⇩ ⇨○⇦ ⇧	🏃
Breakthrough Perspective	*Relentless Focus*	*Blurred Innovation Boundaries*
Software developers don't want to deal with a salesperson, and would much rather service themselves.	Atlassian focuses its suite of products on ones that are well suited to the sort of ground-up adoption that they envisioned—namely software development and collaboration tools.	Atlassian's flagship products—such as Jira and Confluence—are high quality, but the company saves considerably in the way that it manages the sales and marketing of those products.

We've seen this type of costovation in many forms outside of the software industry. At airports with large volumes of business travelers—New York's LaGuardia, Minneapolis, and Toronto, for instance—customers can seat themselves at tables mounted with an iPad and order food and drinks from the tablet at their own convenience. Customers love that they don't wait to flag down a waiter to first bring over the menu and then later get the check; instead, they can order, eat, and be on their way, even if they are in a huge rush. **OTG**, the airport dining operator behind the tablet-food-service innovation, benefits from being able to employ fewer staff and from avoiding bottlenecks at busy times. Hotels and airlines are also playing with ways to help customers get what they want faster and on their own terms, such as self-service check-in kiosks.

WHEN TO USE IT: This strategy is widely applicable across industries from software to hospitality but can deliver particularly large returns where the sales process is traditionally long and complex.

BEST PRACTICES:

■ Cutting sales and marketing can be a seductive proposition, but it is critical to keep a steady eye on your target customer segments and their needs. Take great care to ensure that the changes you are making are going to delight your users—not create new pain points. Keep in mind that this strategy may make great sense for one type of customer but be a Pandora's Box for another.

TRY THIS:

• Draw out a journey map of how your customers interact with your firm, from initial prospecting all the way through to the final sale and post-sale service. It doesn't have to be visual—even just a decision tree will do—but every single interaction should be represented. Then take a step back to assess the value, cost, and hassle of each step.

- Think about your target customers and their attitudes around the traditional sales process. Where is high-touch service needed, and where will low-touch service be enough? Alternatively, think backwards: assume a self-service sales model, and trace back to the kind of customers who would find that better than the traditional sales model. Note that those customers are likely footholds for disruptive innovation.

14. **Tap into people's desires to help others.** Make customers into customer-service agents.

■

Every spring, Americans let out a collective sigh: it's time to file taxes. Time-consuming, complex, and potentially high-stakes if there is an error—there is much to dread about filing your taxes. For many, it is worth the few hundred dollars to outsource the work to an accountant or tax store. But for over 30 million Americans, the chore of tax preparation became easy to do—even *fun*—as a result of **Intuit's** revolutionary TurboTax software.

Much has been written about TurboTax, but one area that we feel is underappreciated is its approach to customer support. Advising others on taxes can be a hairy business, and Intuit didn't want to enter the minefield of giving financial advice. Intuit's solution instead was the TurboTax Live Community, a self-sustaining user collection of enthusiastic TurboTax users and tax experts discussing tax-related questions and problems, and sharing filing tips. Together, they've built a large knowledge base that drives a tremendous amount of search traffic to TurboTax's website. Ingeniously, it also functions like a hands-off online support system for TurboTax, where the community answers its own questions.

TurboTax still invests in a small customer-support team, which users on upgraded plans can call. But for most issues, TurboTax keeps costs down—both for itself and for its users—by having its own user community resolve basic tax and software questions. Other software companies such as **Atlassian** also make use of this tactic, providing spaces for users to discuss how they have used the product and to share advice.

Costovation Traits: Intuit's TurboTax		
Breakthrough Perspective	*Relentless Focus*	*Blurred Innovation Boundaries*
When customers are really excited about a product, they are willing to share their expertise and help others.	To fuel its Live Community, TurboTax focuses on creating an outstanding user experience that inspires users to become evangelists.	The TurboTax Live Community blurs the line between customer and support staff.

WHEN TO USE IT: If you are willing to invest in the resources necessary to grow and sustain a user community, this costovation strategy can empower users, generate leads, grow your presence as a thought leader in the field, and reduce pressure on your customer-service team.

BEST PRACTICES:

■ Focus on creating an excellent user experience for your primary offering. If your offering doesn't excite people in the first place, they won't be inspired to help others.

■ Give your customers a reason to work hard for you. Intuit lets people build profiles so that they earn recognition for their contributions. Some tax accountants use this to boost their visibility and establish themselves as experts.

■ Creating a community—especially a civil and helpful one—is not something that happens overnight. You may need to generate your own content at first and invest resources into monitoring quality and promoting engagement.

TRY THIS:

- Every business has its superusers. Start with them. Ask them to write guest blog posts explaining how they use your offering, as well as to contribute to early discussions.

- Start small and deliver well. Before attempting full-scale rollout, first validate the concept through a small number of frequently asked questions or topics.

15. Price only for the services rendered. Unbundle.

■

After decades in which bundled services were the trend—CNN bundled with Nickelodeon, computers with preloaded software—a new generation of companies is questioning this age-old marketing tactic. Unbundling is usually hailed as a way for businesses to cater to what customers want, though that does not give credit to the fact that it is also a way for companies to isolate the most expensive parts of the business or customer experience—and have customers elect to cut those costs for them.

In the education space, a number of digital-education upstarts are starting to unbundle the university, whose rising tuitions have captured the attention of students, parents, and lawmakers alike. One example is **Minerva**, a venture-capital–backed university founded in 2011. Minerva is focused on educating future leaders in a global context, so a key component of its program is that students move to a new country for each year of their undergraduate experience, choosing between cities like Berlin, Buenos Aires, Seoul, Hyderabad, and Taipei. But there are several elements of the traditional college experience that Minerva daringly cuts—such as college athletics, professor tenure, and a formal campus (students live together in residence halls but take classes online). Because Minerva has eliminated what are usually significant cost-drivers for undergraduate institutions, it is able to set tuition at just $13,000 a year.

Costovation Traits: Minerva		
Breakthrough Perspective	Relentless Focus	Blurred Innovation Boundaries
Higher education doesn't need to be sold in bundles that include everything from gym membership to Wi-Fi to 40 three-credit courses.	Minerva focuses on giving its students broad international education at affordable rates. It enables that by having a digital classroom and cutting some student and teacher benefits.	Minerva pushes the boundaries on *how* the university looks and works.

Capella University took a different tack with unbundling. In 2013, it launched a program called FlexPath, which divorces the notion of the credit hour from the graduate degree. Traditional schools force students to finish a course within a predetermined amount of time (a semester, perhaps, or a quarter), thereby assigning value to the number of hours that a student sits in a classroom listening to a professor. Instead, Capella's FlexPath allows students to choose their own pace. Students are charged one flat tuition fee on a quarterly basis; if they finish their courses early, they can continue on with others without incurring extra costs. This way, smart, motivated students don't have to pay more for what they don't need, which in this case is extra time. Through FlexPath, an MBA might cost less than $10,000 and take less than a year—a far cry from the six-figure price tags from traditional brick-and-mortar institutions.

WHEN TO USE IT: Unbundling can be a helpful response to pain points around pricing. Technology has enabled unbundling in industries and fields where it was once more cumbersome.

BEST PRACTICES:

- Take care to show how unbundling adds value to the customer, not just extra fees. The low-cost airline industry has been maligned for this practice in particular. Maneuvers such as charging $40 to bring a carry-on bag aren't obviously rooted in cost-saving measures for both airline and flyer, so they read as greedy.

TRY THIS:

- Make a full list of the components of your offering. Be comprehensive! Don't forget to include services, both before and after purchasing. Now identify components on your list that fall into either of two categories: 1) are core to your offering, and 2) are used by the majority of your customers. What remains? Consider unbundling options for features or aspects of your business that benefit only a niche segment of your customers (especially if they are drivers of cost for you).

16. Get paid early. Declutter sales channels and lower inventory.

■

The risks of running a ski resort can be literally mountainous. Resorts require massive infrastructure investments like gondolas, grooming machines, and snow-making guns, and then they operate at the mercy of the weather to deliver crowd-drawing snowfall. The industry has been tough in recent years: the total number of U.S. alpine skiers fell from over 10.5 million in the 2010–11 season to 9.8 million in 2016–17, and almost a third of the ski areas in the U.S. are considered to be sunsetting.[12]

And yet there is a lonely bright spot: **Vail Resorts**, the industry behemoth that counts in its portfolio fourteen ski resorts around the world, including Whistler-Blackcomb, Park City, and Beaver Creek. While local ski hills are shutting down, Vail Resorts is in fact growing. And a large part of its success can be chalked up to a dazzling example of costovation in its pricing model.

Vail Resorts centers its business around what it calls the Epic Pass, an incredibly discounted season ticket that grants year-round access to not just one but *all* of its resorts. The Epic Pass is an unbeatable deal for skiers who get out on the mountain more than five days a year; for the 2017–18 season, the Epic Pass sold for $859, while a single-day ticket at Vail retails for around $179. It doesn't matter if you are coming with a group, or have a corporate affiliation, or have a coupon—all skiers are funneled toward one destination only: purchase an Epic Pass. Once skiers are on the mountain, they then spend outsized dollars on dining, lodging, equipment rentals, parking, and ski lessons (which Vail Resorts also owns).

In fall 2017, Vail Resorts sold over 740,000 Epic Passes, netting close to $600 million in nonrefundable ticket fees before the first snowfall of the season.[13] Vail Resorts' pricing innovation allows the organization to lock in a significant part of its budget regardless of future snow conditions, while also putting skiers on an RFID system that creates a treasure trove of data about where its customers ski and who they are skiing with. Meanwhile, skiers rejoice over a new frontier in season-ticket pricing.

Costovation Traits: Vail Resorts		
Breakthrough Perspective	Relentless Focus	Blurred Innovation Boundaries
Instead of relying upon day-of lift ticket sales to cover the cost of operations, Vail Resorts makes the lift ticket the darling attraction that brings the crowds in.	In order to lower the cost of the Epic Pass, Vail Resorts needed to think strategically about how other aspects of the ski experience could generate revenue (such as lodging, ski school, and on-mountain dining).	Mountains may change slowly, but Vail Resorts created a brand new way for skiers to interact with ski resorts. In the process, it revolutionized the ski resort business model.

Here's another example of costovation in the luxury context, this time in fine dining. **Alinea**, a three-Michelin-star restaurant in Chicago, operates a special reservation system that requires customers to pay for their meals online at the time of the booking, which is oftentimes months in advance of the actual meal. This sales innovation has multiple operational advantages. Asking for payment up front whittles no-shows down to an incredible 1.5% rate. It also means that the restaurant can order precise amounts of food, reducing waste. Moving to an online system also means that Alinea can forgo staff for answering reservation inquiries. Ticket prices can be made variable depending on the time and day, in order to help fill tables at low-traffic times like Monday nights. And because reservations can be made only for even numbers of people—tables for two, four, or six—there is never an odd empty seat in the restaurant.

WHEN TO USE IT: This strategy is especially helpful in industries with uneven or difficult-to-predict demand, like in travel and dining. It can also be used as a tool to differentiate a company from competitors.

BEST PRACTICES:

- Careful thought needs to go into determining the "right" price point. Be aware that there may be several right answers. Until 2009, **Dollarama**, a deep discount/value retailer in Canada, sold all its items at just one price point: $1. This drastically simplified in-store operations. Dollarama stores contained no price labels, either on shelves or on individual merchandise. Cash registers only had one button, which was pressed for each item purchased by the customer. Because of the simple pricing structure, it was feasible to manually count inventory instead of having to purchase complex software systems. But after several years, Dollarama found its simple pricing structure suffocating; it was limited in the items it could offer, and inflation put pressure on its margins. Over the next few years, Dollarama introduced seven new price points (topping out at $4), which were launched to great customer praise.

- Give your customer base good reason to participate in your new pricing plan. Chinese smartphone giant **Xiaomi** regularly runs highly anticipated flash events where customers can preorder new phones at fantastically low prices (sometimes during windows as short as fifteen minutes). Bloggers and social-media influencers hype these events, drawing publicity to the company's latest models. Operationally, Xiaomi has a lot to gain: the company begins working with suppliers to build the new phones only once the complete set of orders—and payments—have come in.

TRY THIS:

- Explore what would happen if you charged a lower up-front fee instead of the pricing structure you have now. Even if it sounds like a terrible idea at first, think through the hypothetical pros and cons. How might this new pricing structure change the way your customers viewed the offering? How would it change the way you operated your business? In what ways could it potentially enable you to lower costs?

---

17. **Think twice about real estate.** Examine how location can be an opportunity area for innovation.

■

Coffee shops are firmly entrenched in modern-day South Korean culture—in fact, the average Korean drinks coffee 12.3 times per week (perhaps more often than they eat kimchi!). In 2017, the nation of 50 million people had over 100,000 coffee shops; compare this to the 31,500 that the U.S., a country with six times its population, had in 2015.[14]

To stand out in this cutthroat competitive field, coffee shops in Korea have tried it all: focusing on décor to make the place an escape from the hustle and bustle of city life; pursuing quirky themes like "cat café" or "tent café"; selling beer; providing tables for single customers. **Ediya Coffee**, a popular Korean chain, focuses on low-priced premium coffee—which it can provide by making subprime real estate part of its strategy.

Ediya Coffee stores are generally small shops in less-than-ideal locations—perhaps just a little too far from major tourist attractions and transportation hubs, or a little too tucked into a hidden alley. Here, rent is lower. To bring down rent even more, Ediya runs stores that are significantly smaller than the usual Korean coffee shop. Whereas other chains like A Twosome Place, Caffee Bene, and Angel-in-us open shops measuring over 130 square meters, Ediya prefers shops in the 30-square-meter range. Minimizing shop size encourages takeout, which leads to higher turnover. Ediya Coffee now boasts the largest number of shops for a locally owned Korean brand and was rated by the Korea Consumer Agency as the most reasonably priced coffee in Korea.[15]

Costovation Traits: Ediya Coffee		
👓 *Breakthrough Perspective*	*Relentless Focus*	🏃 *Blurred Innovation Boundaries*
While its competitors focus on making coffee shops full-scale destinations, Ediya saw an opening for take-out coffee in South Korea.	Ediya Coffee is committed to keeping its coffee low-priced—and is willing to accept less-than-ideal real estate to make that happen.	Ediya's coffee beans are high quality, but its real innovation was in giving a fresh look at where coffee was sold.

Businesses in many contexts have found ways to bend the cost curve around real estate and location. Food trucks, for example, live a nomadic life free of rent. **United Apparel**

Liquidators, an off-price high-end fashion retailer that the *New York Times* has called "the best-kept secret in fashion," plants its stores in secondary markets like Hattiesburg, Mississippi and Slidell, Louisiana. In those towns, there is little competition from big retail chains, and image-conscious fashion labels feel okay about "burying the goods" there.[16] **Spirit Halloween**, the U.S.'s leading retailer of Halloween costumes and decorations, signs only three-month retail leases that start in August and end in October. The day after Halloween, all stores close and leftover merchandise is shipped back to central warehouses to put on sale again next year. And **Mary Kay**, the cosmetics company, famously sells its products in the homes of its independent beauty consultants, rather than investing resources in a brick-and-mortar presence.

WHEN TO USE IT: Keep this tactic handy when you are in a crowded category and need to dramatically differentiate yourself, and when the industry or market you are in is accustomed to paying high rents for premium locations.

BEST PRACTICES:

- There are many dimensions to location, and all can be fruitful areas for costovation. In addition to thinking about *where* your assets are, consider also *size* of stores, *number* of stores, and *permanence* of stores.

TRY THIS:

- Start by jotting down your industry's current wisdom about real estate. Perhaps it is assumed that a brick-and-mortar location is a given. Perhaps it is assumed that more locations are better, or that store size is sacred. Now question each individually.

- Engage in a thought exercise: What would a business in your industry have to do to be successful if it were constrained in the location or size of its establishments?

Partnerships with Your Ecosystem

It used to be that businesses lived and thrived within industry silos, where expertise was narrowly focused. But as markets have evolved and advanced, businesses are starting to look a lot more like nature—that is, living in and interacting with richly networked ecosystems comprising suppliers, distributors, customers, competitors, government agencies, and even companies in other categories. The actors in these networks are inextricably linked. As in nature, the actions of one actor can ripple across the networks.

Ecosystems are rich with opportunities for costovation. This final section covers three strategies that involve partnering with other actors in your network to lower costs while focusing on core customer needs.

18. **Share costs in the supply chain.** Apply the sharing economy to your business functions.

■

In 2008, a social-impact–minded Brit named Simon Berry was working in rural Zambia when he observed three things that took his breath away.

The first was that childhood diarrhea—just a pesky nuisance back home in the U.K.—was positively lethal in sub-Saharan Africa. It was the second biggest killer of children aged five and under.

The second was that anti-diarrheal medicines, while very cheap, were consistently hard to find. Patients traveled an average of 7.3 kilometers to reach a health center, but stockrooms were often bare.[17]

The third observation was that while medication was in short supply, Simon never had a problem finding a bottle of soda. Even the tiniest retail stores in the most remote locations in sub-Saharan Africa always had a selection of (warm) soda. You were more likely to encounter a fizzy drink than a reputable source of drinking water—a feat made possible because soda bottlers had carefully nurtured an independent, self-sustaining distribution-and-logistics economy.

Putting these three facts together seemed to write its own solution to a health problem that international aid had long battled. How about piggy-backing diarrhea medication with soda bottles? Through his aptly-named non-profit **ColaLife**, Simon designed special wedge-shaped packaging that could slip medication kits into the empty space around the bottles in a case of soda—without adding any significant new weight. This meant that instead of traveling three or four hours to reach a regional health center, a mother could buy a life-saving antidiarrheal kit at the same local store where she bought a soda, for the price of a dollar.

ColaLife's costovation was to share resources with a business with unexpectedly similar goals, which in this case was to distribute products widely throughout sub-Saharan Africa.

This approach is sometimes referred to as "collaborative distribution" or "shared supply chains."

Costovation Traits: ColaLife		
Breakthrough Perspective	*Relentless Focus*	*Blurred Innovation Boundaries*
Most businesses think that building your own supply chain is an important and necessary act. ColaLife believed that it didn't have to reinvent the wheel.	Though there are many worthwhile health causes that ColaLife could work toward, ColaLife's singular focus was on treating diarrhea in sub-Saharan Africa.	ColaLife invented a nifty triangular package to house its medication, but its signature innovation is in the way the product is distributed—not through its own supply chain, but by piggypacking with soda bottlers.

Here's another example. Distributors know that trucks have two major constraints: space and weight. **Daltile**, which manufactures tiles and stones, was maxing out on its weight capacity long before its trucks were full—in fact, its trucks were only 20% full. **Whirlpool**, on the other hand, was shipping bulky but relatively light objects—by the time their trucks were fully loaded, they were only scraping 20% of the trucks' weight capacity. Combining the two shipments—high-density freight with low-density freight—helped the companies cut 20–30% in their supply-chain costs, as well as reduce their carbon footprint.

The sharing economy is slowly making its way to every industry, with countless startups claiming to be the "Uber" of their industries. But you don't have to wait for that startup to materialize before you can take advantage of the cost-saving benefits of the sharing economy. The benefits can start with a single partnership.

WHEN TO USE IT: This strategy can be a good match for companies that are looking for creative, daring new ways to cut costs—and are capable of building and maintaining unexpected and unconventional partnerships. Over time, this kind of load-sharing may become routine. For example, market-research agencies now often offer "omnibus surveys," where multiple companies share the cost of quantitative surveying when they are seeking quick information from the same demographic group. Instead of each designing, recruiting, and paying for their own survey, survey questions are collected together and asked all at once to the same panel of people.

BEST PRACTICES:

- Although this strategy can work in all industries, it can be especially applicable in asset-intensive ones like telecom. Many cellphone carriers, for instance, share the towers they use to broadcast signals, even while they compete in other respects. This allows them to lower costs on things that customers don't much care about while focusing on what's truly important.

- Start small, with just one partnership focusing on one region and customer. Focus on assets that are not strategic differentiators for your business. Then scale this idea to other parts of the business.

TRY THIS:

- Make a list of the basic functions of your business which are replicated by others. Exclude those that provide a competitive advantage. Then summarize areas of excess capacity that could be used in a partnership. Similarly, identify areas where extra capacity would be quite welcome to your organization. Now, using internal and external contacts, identify companies with common supply chains, customers, and distribution channels.

19. **Seek complements in the value chain.** Match up with organizations with "opposite" supply chains.

■

Company assets can sometimes be unevenly utilized. Trucks drive out full but then make the return journey completely empty; warehouses are built to handle seasonal peaks but then sit unused during the lows; specialized manufacturing lines work in overdrive when demand is forecast but are wasteful otherwise. Many companies regard seasonality as an inevitable and unavoidable part of the business, but it doesn't have to be so. This strategy involves pairing organizations with "opposite" capacity needs, which can give new life to underutilized assets.

Rocky's Beverages is a Chicago-based startup that manufactures the world's first caffeine-infused club soda. Like most any startup, it's a lean operation, and it didn't want to commit to a long warehouse lease while it was still figuring things out. Meanwhile, a Christmas-decorations company owned plenty of warehouse space but only made full use of it in the months leading up to the holidays.

Instead of accepting this seasonality as a fact of life, the holiday-decorations company saw an opportunity. It had excess storage in its warehouses during the spring and summer, and it could cut a sublease to Rocky's in lieu of

letting the space lay vacant and unused. This was a mutually beneficial relationship: the decorations company was
able to recoup some of its sunk warehouse costs, and the
beverage-maker received access to much-needed warehouse
space, particularly in hotter months when people consume
more beverages. Moreover, Rocky's didn't have to pay for a
day more of rent than it needed and didn't have to invest in
its own warehouse workers or forklifts.

The beverage company and the decorations retailer have
what we call "opposite" capacity needs, which makes a partnership between the two truly symbiotic. In this instance, this
match was made by a platform called **Flexe**, although partnerships like this can be successfully created without a broker.

Costovation Traits: Christmas Decorations Company		
Breakthrough Perspective	Relentless Focus	Blurred Innovation Boundaries
Seasonality doesn't have to be an inevitable and unavoidable part of doing business.	The company focused on its warehouses, which glaringly stood empty for a significant part of the year.	This innovation of sharing warehousing space occurred deep inside the company's supply chain.

Let's look at how this logic applies to intangibles—in this
case, money transfers. **TransferWise** saves costs on international money transfers by matching users who each have
the currencies the other desires. A simple swap then takes
place. For example, if someone wants to convert pounds to
euros, TransferWise's technology finds someone who wants
to transfer money in the other direction (euros into pounds).
The system automatically matches the currency flows at the
real mid-market exchange rate and then pays out from the
local euro or pound account, meaning the money never

actually moves across borders. This way customers avoid traditional banking fees and don't lose money by transferring at an unfair rate.

WHEN TO USE IT: This strategy was born out of the pain points seasonality creates, but has applications to industries with both tangible and intangible assets. A key sign that this costovation technique might be appropriate is having a predictable volume of underutilized assets.

BEST PRACTICES:

- Complementing can occur up and down the supply chain. Major areas to look at include warehouses, distribution centers, and trucking (particularly backhauling).
- Don't forget to look internally—sometimes a great complement already exists inside your organization, between different lines of business. These collaborative partnerships can be quicker to set up and less risky than working with outside parties.

TRY THIS:

- Examine your business for areas where capacity is underutilized. Where are empty backhauls most common? How much warehouse space is available during the off-season?

- Identify companies with contrasting demand or seasonality. Pay special attention to organizations or industries that are rapidly growing.

- Look internally for opportunities to collaborate with different products or groups within your organization.

20. Treat your suppliers like customers. Grow your accounts by helping your value chain become more productive.

■

For decades, **Li & Fung** has been the go-to company for helping Western brands like Tommy Hilfiger and Abercrombie & Fitch connect with Asian factories to manufacture their products. But after many years of runaway success, the company was facing difficulties in sustaining the growth rates that its shareholders were used to. Li & Fung knew it needed to take a different approach.

Li & Fung's key realization was that its services were only as strong as its partners. If one of its partner factories failed to produce, Li & Fung suffered. Its solution was to look upstream at their suppliers and do what it could to improve *their* businesses. Treating them more like customers than vendors, they asked: what can we do to help them become more productive? What are the jobs they are trying to get done, and what gets in the way of accomplishing them?

Li & Fung discovered that factories in Bangladesh, for instance, struggled with getting trade financing—so it committed to helping them find credit so that they could finance their own purchases and inventory. For factories in China and India, Li & Fung used its operations expertise to help them become leaner, more efficient, and less wasteful, with the result that in some factories the efforts helped to raise productivity by as much as 90% over six months.[18] This meant that Li & Fung's partner factories could take on more projects per year, and the company's Western clients received better quality goods, faster.

Eventually, Li & Fung bundled these vendor-support services into a new business model, which not only created a new revenue stream but also strengthened the quality of supply chains for its core business.

Costovation Traits: Li & Fung		
Breakthrough Perspective	Relentless Focus	Blurred Innovation Boundaries
Li & Fung reframed the way it approached its suppliers—seeing them less as vendors and more as enablers of their own growth.	Li & Fung focuses on its suppliers, treating them as if they were a class of customers of their own.	In looking for ways to grow and scale its business, Li & Fung looked beyond the parts of the business that its traditional customers could see, and it explored new thinking around its own supply chain.

Strengthening your value chain helps make your own business more efficient—and, in the case of Li & Fung, this even became a revenue-producing business unit.

WHEN TO USE IT: This strategy is widely applicable, but it is an especially relevant approach for larger organizations that have scale advantages that their suppliers do not. These companies can use their position to empower their suppliers in new ways.

BEST PRACTICES:

■ Use the same market-research techniques you use to assess customers on your suppliers. We particularly like the "jobs to be done" line of thinking first popularized by Harvard Business School Professor Clayton Christensen, which identifies root motivations, forces that drive behavior, obstacles that get in the way of achieving goals, and pain points.

■ Start small, working closely with one or two suppliers to finesse a new program before rolling it out to others.

➡️ | **TRY THIS:**

- Identify a set of suppliers that you wish to develop tighter relationships with. Find out what jobs these suppliers are trying to get done, and what gets in the way. This information is usually best elicited via one-on-one interviews. Then explore how helping the supplier achieve its jobs to be done can fit within your company's competencies and strategic objectives.

/ part four /

the greater context

chapter 6

•

Diagnostic: Seven Signs That Your Industry Is Ripe for Costovation

"It's always about timing," *Vogue* editor Anna Wintour once said. "If it's too soon, no one understands. If it's too late, everyone's forgotten."

As innovation consultants, we often receive "when" questions. When will this new market take off? How long do we have before others catch on? When will the timing be just right to launch this new idea? When is costovation appropriate for us?

No one can predict the future with much specificity. But there are indicators that can foreshadow what is to come. In this section, we share seven signs that often characterize industries before a costovation hits the market. If one or more of the following applies to your industry or category, buckle up: change is coming, to be led by you or one of your competitors.

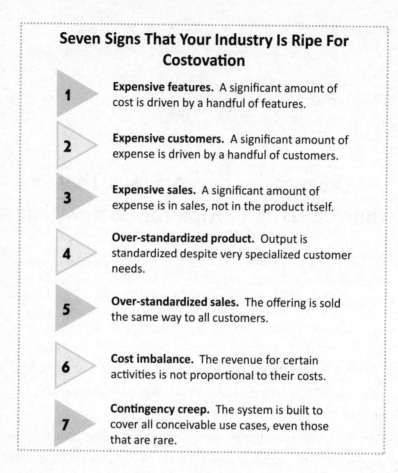

Seven Signs That Your Industry Is Ripe For Costovation

1   **Expensive features.** A significant amount of cost is driven by a handful of features.

2   **Expensive customers.** A significant amount of expense is driven by a handful of customers.

3   **Expensive sales.** A significant amount of expense is in sales, not in the product itself.

4   **Over-standardized product.** Output is standardized despite very specialized customer needs.

5   **Over-standardized sales.** The offering is sold the same way to all customers.

6   **Cost imbalance.** The revenue for certain activities is not proportional to their costs.

7   **Contingency creep.** The system is built to cover all conceivable use cases, even those that are rare.

SIGN #1: Expensive features. *A significant amount of cost is driven by a handful of features.*

The tendency for companies over time is to add, add, and add—new programs, extra features, deluxe options—and to steer clear of cutting or subtracting. Taking features away almost always hurts some constituency, so it's easier to keep everyone friendly through piling things on instead. Not all additions are equal, however. While some truly help to differentiate the company, others can be significant drivers of cost. And when expensive *optional* features become expensive *permanent* features, it's time to sit up straight. This is an opportunity for someone to dramatically reduce costs by eliminating a relatively small part of the value proposition.

We'll illustrate this with a grocery example. Traditional supermarkets like Kroger or Safeway tend to pride themselves on having a wide selection, which makes them a one-stop shop not just for food, but also for paper products, kitchenware, liquor, holiday cards, you name it. The trade-off is that maintaining such a varied selection can be enormously costly. Stores and distribution centers need to be bigger to house all the goods. Employees have to scurry around to keep large stores well stocked and organized. Buyers for Wal-Mart have to keep track of 150,000 different products, up from 9,000 at the average supermarket in 1975. And consumers don't necessarily benefit. A 2014 survey by Consumer Reports found that almost a third of shoppers said that they were overwhelmed by the information they had to process to make a buying decision. Intrigued by that figure, researchers turned around and looked at the grocery shelves themselves. They counted nine varieties of Pringles potato chips, 25 formulations of Head & Shoulders shampoo, and 74 kinds of Campbell's condensed soup.[1]

Noting how the pursuit of selection had led supermarkets to twist their supply chains into knots, the global grocery chain Lidl decided to take a different approach. Instead of having the twenty-five to thirty aisles typical in a supermarket, the German-based company features just six. By the time customers have reached the end of the first aisle, they'll have typically completed about 80% of their shopping. Giving customers just two pickle options to choose from rather than a dozen translates into simplified inventory as well as increased buying power from suppliers, and this ultimately means that shoppers can unlock

35–40% savings on their weekly groceries.[2] For Lidl's target shoppers, that discount is absolutely worth the trade-off in selection.

Costco plays a similar game—no one goes to Costco for its toothpaste selection, but the toothpaste they do carry is reliably well-priced. The selection at a typical Costco warehouse features about 4,000 fast-selling items, compared to 80,000 at Target. Both Lidl and Costco zoomed in on a cost-driving feature—in this case, having a wide selection in the grocery business—and dismantled it to great cost savings.

Costovation response: Isolate the features that drive up costs. Cut back or find ways to improve their return on investment.

SIGN #2: Expensive customers. *A significant amount of expense is driven by a handful of customers.*

Sometimes costs are driven not by certain features, but by a small segment of customers who have complex needs, demand extra care, or require different processes. Being able to identify and isolate these customers is key not only for reducing overall costs, but also for uncovering opportunities to serve customers in better, more targeted ways.

Pundits have for years proclaimed the coming disruption of higher education, often at the hand of technologies like Massive Open Online Courses (MOOCs) or trends such as underemployment among graduates. Many colleges will indeed merge or shutter their doors in the next decade, but their killer may be stealthier: poor attrition rates. The most expensive students are the ones who drop out and need to be replaced. A 2013 study by the Educational Policy Institute found that the cost of acquiring one undergraduate student was $5,460, and that the average college loses several million dollars a year from retention issues, largely from lost tuition revenue.[3]

American Military University—a for-profit online learning institution—hasn't felt the same heat. This is in large part because it focuses on a customer segment that is known for determination and grit: active members of the military and veterans. Because its retention rates are higher, and because this is a very targeted sales channel, American Military University can afford to charge less tuition than its peers ($270 per undergraduate credit hour, compared to as much as $400 per credit hour at a comparable online institution).

In higher education, students who are at high risk of dropping out can command an outsized proportion of a school's focus. We see a similar phenomenon in healthcare, where just 1% of U.S. patients account for 22.7% of total U.S. healthcare costs.[4] Take a good look at your customer base. Which subsets of customers drive expense for your organization?

Costovation response: Adjust your approach to more efficiently serve the "expensive" customers or make the strategic decision to focus on other populations.

SIGN #3: Expensive sales. *A significant amount of expense is in sales, not in the product itself.*

The third indicator of an industry that is ready for costovation is a long and complex sales process. When the sales force drives significant internal costs, perhaps more than the product itself is worth, an organization becomes vulnerable to costovation—not necessarily in the product, but rather in the way that the offering is sold.

Cameron Hughes, a wine expert and entrepreneur, did just that when he started re-shaping the wine market in 2001. "I've been in the wine business my whole life," he said. "And what I've discovered is that wine does not cost a lot to make. It costs a lot to sell."[5] Much of the expense in the wine market comes from the U.S.'s three-tier liquor distribution system; by the time a bottle has passed through distributors, wholesalers, and retailers, it's not unusual to see markups of 200% or more.[6] Excess wine inventory is sold off on the bulk market, where it is mixed together with lesser wines into anonymous blends.

This long, convoluted sales chain produces a fantastic costovation opportunity. Hughes travels the world buying up extra inventory from world-class wine producers—a few cases here and a few lots there. Then he relabels the bottles under his company's own name, taking care to shield the original winery's identity. The wineries are happy to unload their unsold product (and relieved that they don't have to compromise their brands through discounting). Consumers, meanwhile, are thrilled to get their hands on a $100 Napa cabernet for just $30 a bottle. Cameron Hughes Wine runs a premium business with exceptionally low costs: it doesn't own any wineries or vineyards, and it cuts out middlemen by selling only through Costco and its website.

Innovation activities are too seldom applied to marketing and sales channels, but when they are, the impact can be tremendous. As you examine your industry, check whether the traditional sales channel may be creating conditions for a costovation to break in.

Costovation response: Find daring new ways to circumvent traditional sales channels, and costovate the way the offering is sold.

SIGN #4: Over-standardized product. *Output is standardized despite very specialized customer needs.*

A fourth sign of a costovation opportunity lies in the offering itself. Keep an eye out for instances where output is overly standardized, forcing customers with many unique needs to make do with just one offering. In these situations, there will likely be a subset of customers who are under-satisfied with the current options. They will be the first to line up for an alternative that more directly addresses their contexts and the jobs they are trying to get done in their lives, even if it doesn't deliver on every kind of performance dimension imaginable.

Let's jump back to education for a brief example, although this time we'll discuss grade school. For the past twenty years, the average cost of private-school tuition has steadily grown at a rate that is higher than inflation, to the point where $35,000 is the average yearly rate for private schooling in New England. Families have noticed: across the U.S., private-school enrollment from middle-income families has halved in the same amount of time.[7]

These intense marketplace pressures have spurred a range of innovations and costovations. Among them is a new micro school in Providence, Rhode Island, brought to fruition by education entrepreneur Michael Goldstein (whose past work includes Bridge International Academies, profiled in Section 2). The micro school aims to offer high-quality education at half the usual cost of private schooling, which is made possible by simplifying the school down to its most important components. There are no administrators—just teachers. And most importantly, there is no extra programming or after-school classes—just the core subjects, taught very well.

This micro school is perfect for parents who are willing to take on the work of finding supplemental activities themselves. For some families, this is a dream: they can choose extracurricular activities that pivot around their interests, rather than a uniform set of activities passed down through the decades. The micro school takes what is often a very standardized product— grade-school education—and reinvents it to both cut costs for parents *and* make it more flexible.

Costovation response: Zoom in on the customer subsets that are dissatisfied or under-satisfied with current solutions. They are your foothold to disruptive innovation.

SIGN #5: Over-standardized sales. *The offering is sold the same way to all customers.*

Many businesses sell their offering to all their customers in the same way. This is logistically simpler to manage, and oftentimes companies haven't had the time to question whether there is a better way. But not all customers have the same needs. When an offering is sold the same way to all customers, companies leave an opportunity open for someone to target a certain subset of the population and sell to them in ways that perfectly address their needs.

In the late 2000s, the medical device maker Medtronic had the great foresight to realize that its profitable heart pacemaker and defibrillator business was in danger of being disrupted. Medtronic's cardiac-rhythm-device business was based partly around providing top-of-the-market technical assistance and training, and this attention to detail had helped the company soar for decades. But that high level of service overshot the needs of a significant segment of its customers: hospitals that were mature in their use of pacemakers and defibrillators, consistent in their purchasing patterns, and no longer in need of training and other after-sale services. This group of customers was vulnerable to poaching from competitors, especially in European hospitals where the costs of caring for an aging population were escalating beyond relatively static budgets.

In response, Medtronic established NayaMed, an economy option for European hospitals driven to lower their costs. NayaMed focuses on physicians who are sophisticated in their understanding of cardiac devices and no longer need to be marketed to; accordingly, NayaMed cut out traveling sales teams and instead sells its products online. It also makes its training virtual rather than live, since these physicians already knew how to use these devices. And to further improve hospital efficiency, NayaMed focuses on self-setting pacemakers that adjust to a patient's heartbeat and largely configure themselves. This reduces the amount of time that physicians need to spend tinkering with dozens of parameters on the devices. NayaMed didn't just cut, though: the company added sophisticated inventory-management services, reasoning that these hospitals bought largely through purchasing managers who would care about these features in ways that physicians do not.

These weren't easy decisions for the company, which had high-end service baked into its DNA. After all, it had *invented* the pacemaker. But the move allowed Medtronic to stay relevant for a class of customers it had been leaving by the wayside, extinguishing opportunities for disruptive, low-end competitors to grab a foothold.

Costovation response: Identify customer segments whose needs are being underserved or overserved by the traditional sales mechanism. Design a new approach that is tailored to meet their core needs (and does not overshoot them).

SIGN #6: Cost imbalance. *The revenue for certain activities is not proportional to their costs.*

The sixth situation to watch out for occurs when the costs and revenues for certain activities are not proportional—that is, activities are either over- or underpriced relative to their costs. These are opportunities to either adjust pricing or re-examine expensive features.

McDonald's has made the most of a cost imbalance in the coffee market. In the U.S. coffee league, Dunkin' Donuts and Starbucks are the top rivals. Both sell food—doughnuts, scones, breakfast sandwiches—but the real margins come from their beverages. At Starbucks, a $7 cup of ultra-premium coffee is rumored to cost the company only $1.30 to produce. At Dunkin', industry experts estimate mark-ups are as high as 95%.[8]

McDonald's takes a different tack. Instead of raking in profits on coffee products like Dunkin' and Starbucks do, McDonald's prices its coffee way lower, starting at $1. This is more in line with its costs and has the magical effect of bringing people into its stores, especially in the mornings. There, McDonald's uses its superior economics with its regular food offerings to make its profit.

As you take a look around your industry, keep an eye out for categories where margins are traditionally cushy, and explore ways that you can subvert them.

Costovation response: Stand out in the industry by adjusting pricing to accurately reflect the value being delivered.

SIGN #7: Contingency creep. *The system is built to cover all conceivable use cases, even those that are rare.*

The notion of being fully, exhaustingly comprehensive can be seductive: Who doesn't want to become a one-stop shop? But not everyone can—or should—aspire to be as omnipresent and all-knowing. Being prepared for rare-use cases can be simply overkill for many contexts. For industries and categories where being comprehensive is the norm, there can be incredible costo-vation opportunities to be had.

When was the last time you went to a picture-frame store? If you're under the age of forty, you probably can't remember, because you never have. Frame shops can feel like old art bou-tiques: the walls are covered in *thousands* of pieces of frame op-tions, the tables are covered with hundreds of mat options, and salespeople are eager to engage with you about the "grade of materials" you seek. No matter what you bring in to frame, be it a digital photo print or a diploma or a treasured pair of baby socks, you can rest assured that these professionals can design a solution for you. Of course, you'll pay handsomely for it. Pricing at framing shops can be completely opaque, quickly rising into hundreds if not thousands of dollars for a custom project.

One of the major reasons why custom framing costs so much is because the emphasis on offering every imaginable type of molding makes it impossible for shops to take advantage of econ-omies of scale. Instead, frame shops have to place small orders for materials as projects come in. This is also why it can take weeks for framing projects to complete.

Framebridge, a startup with more than $37 million in venture capital to its name, takes a different approach. Instead of trying to offer limitless framing options, it focuses on just the few dozen most popular looks. Customers order online, either mailing in their art or uploading it to the company's website, and receive their fully framed pieces within three days for between $39 and $139. By limiting its framing options, Framebridge makes the framing and decorating process easy and inexpensive—so easy that one third of the company's customers are first-time framers.[9] Along the way, the company is proving to the world that the fragmented framing market may be much bigger than originally imagined.

Hospitals are another example of a context built to satisfy every possible situation. There is certainly a need for a service like this— humans do find themselves in the most baffling and inexplicable of health situations—but it's not the case that *every* hospital needs to be so robustly prepared. By cutting low-volume, high-cost features, providers can bring down overall healthcare costs while truly excelling in a smaller number of activities. That's what Minute Clinic does: it focuses on light-touch health needs such as treating minor illnesses and injuries, monitoring chronic health conditions, and administering vaccinations and physicals—all for low, clearly defined up-front prices and with minimal wait time. Any issues graver than the common cold or a sinus infection are beyond Minute Clinic's scope and referred to other institutions.

Costovation response: Pick your battles and focus on what is the most impactful.

––––––

These seven signs are like early raindrops preceding a costovation storm. If any of these signs sounds like an apt description of your company or industry—and *especially* if multiple ones ring true—take a hard look at how costovation can change the playing field for you. If you don't, it may only be a matter of time before someone else does.

CHAPTER SUMMARY

Is costovation coming for your industry? Here are seven signs to keep an eye out for. If one or more applies to your context, stay vigilant: you may be in a great position to use costovation to accelerate growth and solidify market position.

1. **Expensive features.** A significant amount of cost is driven by a handful of features. *Costovation response:* Isolate the cost-drivers, and either eliminate the associated features or find ways to improve their return on investment.

2. **Expensive customers.** A significant amount of expense is driven by a handful of customers. *Costovation response:* Adjust your strategy for the "expensive" customers, or make the decision to focus on other populations.

3. **Expensive sales.** A significant amount of expense is in sales, not in the product itself. *Costovation response:* Find daring new ways to circumvent traditional sales channels, and costovate the way the offering is sold.

4. **Over-standardized product.** Output is standardized despite very specialized customer needs. *Costovation response:* Zoom in on the customer subsets who are dissatisfied or under-satisfied with current solutions. They are your foothold to disruptive innovation.

5. **Over-standardized sales.** The offering is sold the same way to all customers. *Costovation response:* Identify customer segments whose needs are being underserved or overserved by the traditional sales mechanism. Design a new approach that is tailored to meet their core needs (and does not overshoot them).

6. **Cost imbalance.** The revenue for certain activities is not proportional to their costs. *Costovation response:* Stand out in the industry by adjusting pricing to accurately reflect the value being delivered.

7. **Contingency creep.** The system is built to cover all conceivable use cases, even those that are rare. *Costovation response:* Pick your battles, and focus on what is the most impactful.

chapter 7

•

How Costovation Fits in with the Rest of Your Strategy

As we pored over hundreds of examples of costovation, we were surprised by the sheer diversity of ways that companies had put it to use. Many use costovation to play offense, such as to differentiate themselves, redefine the industry on their own terms, or find new oxygen in markets that have otherwise been filled to the brim. This is what initially drew us to costovation—we were curious about companies like Planet Fitness and Picard that were rocking their industries with a laser focus on their customers' needs while keeping costs low.

We also found that companies were using costovation strategies in quieter ways, such as to build defenses and protect themselves against competitive and macro forces. Sometimes these companies were actively under threat, but other times companies were planning ahead for times of economic trouble, instability, or coming adversities that could affect their target customer base.

Below are six ways that companies have integrated costovation into both their growth and defensive strategies, and how you can do the same.

Playing Offense with Costovation

1. At its core, costovation is a way to *seize unaddressed markets.* Vast ranks of customers are barely touched by products and services today, their needs unmet and in many cases unknown. Costovation is a tool for creating and penetrating markets that didn't previously exist.

   For example, the legal industry is ill-famed for being overly complicated and expensive, especially for small-business owners who are also juggling many other aspects of running a company. Unable to afford traditional legal services (and eager to get back to working on the core of the business), many entrepreneurs forgo professional legal advice, instead reading online articles and relying on word-of-mouth advice.

Enter LegalZoom, a self-service website that creates standardized contracts for individuals and small-business owners. LegalZoom's range of services is limited mostly to incorporation papers, trademarks, and wills. But it provides those at exceedingly low costs, like $149 to set up an LLC. Customers can also purchase subscriptions for unlimited attorney consultations for around $360 per year, a price that many lawyers charge for just one hour's work. By relentlessly focusing on a small number of offerings and tackling the obstacles that hinder potential buyers, LegalZoom opened up consumption of legal services for a legion of customers who wouldn't have acted otherwise.

Remember: In addition to studying customers, you need to identify and investigate individuals who are *not* consuming the category of the products you sell at all. What is getting in the way of their becoming users? Perhaps they have a different set of jobs that they are looking to get done, or perhaps some other obstacle—like price, access, or knowledge—is holding them back. Challenge those barriers.

2. One of the most common ways that we've seen costovation used is to *disrupt an industry*. Industry disruptors are so named because they often start out so modest that they catch deep-pocketed incumbents by surprise.

   Dollar Shave Club, for instance, shook up the razor industry—a market that was growing thick with ever-fancier razor options—with its direct-to-consumer model. The online company sends no-frills disposable blades to subscribers for as little as $3 per month, circumventing retail middlemen by using the postal system for easy distribution. The actual production of the razor is outsourced to a South Korean manufacturer, leaving Dollar Shave Club free to concentrate on marketing and customer service, and to be unburdened by heavy asset investments. The razor giants initially wrote off Dollar Shave Club because they couldn't fathom that people would be content with such a basic product. They were wrong. Within just five years of its inception, Dollar Shave Club became too large to ignore, and in 2016 Unilever purchased the company for a stunning $1 billion.

Remember: The term "disruption" is often overapplied to anything novel. Clayton Christensen—the Harvard Business School professor who coined the term—specified that industry disruptors are those who target *overlooked* or *overshot* customers and usage occasions, instead offering lower prices, greater convenience, or totally new types of performance. True disruptors start on the low end of the customer spectrum, where industry giants often have blind spots. Costovation is a formula for addressing those underserved customers effectively.

3. Costovation can also be a winning formula for companies seeking to *enter an emerging market.* Creating long-lasting businesses in emerging markets often requires much more than simply offering a cheaper version of premium products sold elsewhere. Rather, emerging markets typically need distinctly new approaches.

This is the mindset that Nathan Eagle adopted when he founded Jana, the largest provider of free Internet in emerging markets. In emerging markets, mobile phones are nearing ubiquity, thanks in large part due to pricing as low as $20 and the proliferation of mobile infrastructure (over 70% of the world's population lives within reach of at least a 3G

Internet signal). Mobile data, however, is dearly expensive. In fact, almost half of all smartphone users in these markets do not have a data plan at all.[1]

For the millions of people who have a phone but who cannot afford data access, Jana helps make that final connection to the Internet. Jana offers a special mobile web browser that provides free data access in exchange for viewing occasional advertisements. By shifting costs from those who cannot pay for broadband to those who are more than happy to, Jana opens up the Internet to 4.56 billion people around the world. The appeal is clear—Jana's mobile browser very rapidly became the fastest-growing one ever launched.

Remember: When approaching emerging markets, it is vital to think beyond merely offering a stripped-down version of what you would sell in a developed market. Designing for these markets should be rooted in a deep understanding of your customers. You may be surprised by the trade-offs that they are willing to make, and how those trade-offs counter norms and industry assumptions found elsewhere.

Playing Defense with Costovation

1. Especially for more established businesses, costovation is an important technique for *defending market position against low-price competitors, or the possible threat of one.* According to the theory of disruptive innovation, companies at some point eventually run out of room at the top of their markets. They've already captured the most profitable customers and have provided the features that the market really wants. This is when

companies are most vulnerable to disruption from below. To continue growing, companies need to consider "great leaps downward" that reduce cost while improving accessibility and convenience. If they don't do it, someone else will.

Automaker General Motors did just that when it launched Wuling Motors, a joint venture in China with SAIC Motor. While GM operates luxury brands at home in North America, its approach in China is comparatively down-market. Instead of prestigious vehicles with top-of-the-line interiors and the finest in motor technologies, Wuling offers a series of simple vans. The vehicles meet only minimum government construction standards. Interiors are hard plastic, and air conditioning is an optional upgrade. But the vehicles are designed to excel on the bumpy road conditions common outside major Chinese cities, and they help drivers efficiently squeeze past others in narrow, crowded streets. Wuling's vehicles also qualify for efficient-vehicle government subsidies, making car ownership affordable for millions of China's less affluent rural residents. With this basic but thoughtfully designed product, Wuling gives GM a platform in China and protects the company from being disrupted by low-cost automakers in the region.

Remember: It's important to continually take stock of where and how your organization may be vulnerable to disruptive innovation and low-priced competitors, and then to formulate a preemptive response. Below, we list six indicators of an industry that is at risk of disruption:

- Have industry offerings been steadily improving for a
  long time?
- Do customers think older versions of a product are
  good enough?

- Do new products struggle to attain a price premium?
- Do some customers avoid complicated features or lack the training to use them?
- Are there pockets of consumers who don't consume your category at all?
- Is there space to simplify the offering for a segment of the market?

2. Costovation is also a way to *stay on top of a market amid great macroeconomic, population, and demographic change.* The answer to these pressures is not always to run upmarket, or even to economize down to nothing. Sometimes it's best to reinvent the offering.

In the U.S., healthcare providers are being squeezed by a storm of macro events. Complex treatments and chronic diseases are pushing up the cost of therapies. Care is fragmented among a burgeoning army of specialist physicians. Changing legislation creates uncertainty about compensation structures. Administrative costs in this multifaceted system can be enormous; in 2013, Duke University Hospital had 1,300 billing clerks for 900 hospital beds.[2]

ENT Institute navigates these changes by operating a different business model than its hospital competitors. The company is an Atlanta-based medical network with sixteen locations to treat ear, nose, and throat ailments. Instead of offering a full range of services, it eliminates money-losing departments such as the emergency room and focuses its services instead around the more profitable operating room. This allows ENT Institute to charge 20% to 80% less than competitive medical facilities, even while paying doctors more than they could earn in a regular private practice. A tonsillectomy for an adult, for instance, costs about $2,300, compared with a national average of about $4,000 from a hospital or a hospital-owned surgery center.

Remember: Times of industry turmoil and churn are great opportunities for costovation. Stay ahead by keeping tabs on macro movements and trends, extrapolating their effects on your industry and company, and projecting different scenarios. Use this pressure to question long-held assumptions in your industry and to identify opportunities for costovation.

3. Even in economies that are booming, there are always both winners and losers. Over the past four decades, average wages in the U.S. have barely kept pace with inflation, despite increasing worker productivity and overall positive economic gain.[3] When you look beyond averages, the numbers show dramatically uneven growth: while incomes for the top 1% have grown 138% since 1979, incomes for the bottom 90% have grown just 15% in the same amount of time.[4] The rapid growth of automation and artificial intelligence may augment this trend still more. Innovation needs to *address those who aren't gaining economically,* as well as to *build up safeguards against downturns.*

    That's what upscale department retailer Nordstrom did when it launched Nordstrom Rack in the 1970s as a clearance outlet. Rack stores help Nordstrom manage unsold inventory, while also providing a different price point that makes the chain accessible to a new segment of shoppers. Through this dual-pronged strategy that caters both to high-end and budget-minded shoppers, Nordstrom insulates itself from recessions and turbulent economies while still pushing forward on its premium business. Today, Nordstrom Rack contributes

40% of Nordstrom's overall sales, and it is growing faster than the core business. Nordstrom's competitors noticed: in 1990, Saks Fifth Avenue followed suit with its line of Off 5th stores, and there are now twice as many Off 5th stores as there are regular Saks locations.

Remember: It's important to keep an eye on those who are not gaining economically, and even in times of economic prosperity, make sure you have a plan for inevitable downward cycles.

	Strategy	Example
Playing Offense with Costovation	Seize markets that are overlooked by current products and services	LegalZoom opened up consumption for a group of customers who wouldn't have purchased legal services otherwise.
	Disrupt an industry	Dollar Shave Club disrupted the razor industry with its direct-to-consumer model selling no-frills disposable razors to subscribers for as little as $3 per month.
	Enter an emerging market	Jana delivers free Internet to millions of people around the world who cannot afford mobile data, but who are happy to view advertisements in exchange for Internet access.
Playing Defense with Costovation	Defend market position against low-priced competitors	General Motors protects itself against low-end competitors in the Chinese market through its joint venture Wuling Motors, which makes plastic-seated, no-frills vans that drive well on narrow, bumpy roads and qualify for low-emission subsidies.
	Stay on top amid great macroeconomic, population, and demographic change	Atlanta-based ENT Institute navigates an increasingly expensive healthcare landscape by focusing on the more profitable operating room and cutting away money-losing features like the emergency room.
	Address those who aren't gaining economically, and build up safeguards against downturns	Nordstrom's clearance outlet Nordstrom Rack helps the company serve both high-end and budget-minded clientele and keep shoppers within the Nordstrom franchise during economic turbulence.

The Aftermath: Preparing for your Competitors' Responses

As you move forward, it is important to think through what competitive responses your successful costovation may trigger, and to prepare for them.

For a cautionary tale, take a look at business-class–only airlines, a model which sprung up in popularity in the early 2000s. One of these entrepreneurs, Dave Spurlock, was the spry head of strategy at British Airways. He noticed that his company made huge profits in its trans-Atlantic business-class service and saw a market opportunity to provide upmarket service for significantly less. In 2004, he left BA and launched his own airline, dubbed Eos Airlines, that would focus on all-business travel between New York City and London at a relatively cut-rate price. But British Airways, Virgin Atlantic, and others who had much to lose were not just going to let Spurlock go unanswered. They had the flexibility to cut fares on those routes, and swiftly they did, starving Eos for business just as the economy began to soften and fuel prices spiked. In 2008, Eos filed for bankruptcy.

The trouble with Eos was that its pricing was only marginally better than competitors. It was not like Southwest Airlines, which uprooted the traditional business practices of an airline in order to offer fares that others simply could not match. Eos's innovations were surface level. Worse still, the company did not have a good answer ready for how it would circumnavigate its legacy competitors' robust loyalty programs and frequent flight schedules.

One of the best ways to ward off competitors is by ensuring that your innovations go deep into the business. Extend your innovation activities beyond surface-level product changes that are visible to all, and tinker in areas like your supply chain, operations, marketing, and customer service. Doing so leads to business models that are not only lean and cutting edge, but also devilishly tricky to copy.

Launching an innovation can be like planning a wedding: it's easy to get caught up in the fun details of the party and become distracted from laying the groundwork for what happens afterwards (a lifelong commitment). As you move along the innovation journey, think about the different scenarios that may occur once you launch your costovation, and be sure that you are prepared for each.

––––––––––

The goal of this chapter has been to show you that costovation, just like innovation, is a flexible tool. It is not just for the good times, although it can certainly help extend the cheer; likewise, it is much more than just an austerity measure for economic slumps.

In the next and final chapter, we'll leave you with a five-step checklist of what you can do today to get started on costovation immediately.

CHAPTER SUMMARY

When should an organization use costovation, and how does it fit in with our broader strategy? Costovation is exceptionally versatile and has been used to great success both as a tool for growth (for playing "offense") and as a means of protection (for playing "defense").

For companies seeking growth and expansion, costovation can be a way to:

☞ Seize markets that are overlooked by current products and services.

☞ Disrupt an industry.

☞ Enter an emerging market.

For companies that are concerned about protecting their hard-won assets and market position, costovation can be used to:

☞ Defend market position against low-priced competition.

☞ Stay on top of macroeconomic, population, and demographic change.

☞ Address those who aren't gaining economically, and build up safeguards against downturns.

Checklist for Getting Started

It's Monday Morning. What Do You Do?

STEP 1: Gather lessons learned from past innovation efforts and get into a mindset of innovation.

Learn from the past:

❑ Identify why your past attempts at business-model innovation have failed, succeeded, or never gotten off the ground.

❑ Do the same for your competition.

❑ From these experiences, pinpoint any organizational, sales-channel, strategic, or other barriers that may get in the way in the future. Craft plans to bypass them.

Adopt a mindset of innovation:

❑ Make sure that people relevant to this project have a strong grasp of common innovation behaviors (e.g., uncovering market trends, questioning what they think they know, embracing an attitude of flexibility and adaptability, networking outside their fields to find inspiration and to challenge preconceptions). Ensure that they also have access to innovation tools and reference materials.

❑ Provide cover for those who are bold enough to take on tough innovation challenges. Stipulate that failure will not devastate their careers, so long as they use appropriate innovation behaviors.

Are you ready for the next step?

❏ We understand why innovation has failed or succeeded in the past.

❏ We have crafted a plan for overcoming obstacles that currently stand in the way of innovation.

❏ We understand how we need to behave to be innovative.

❏ The organization is ready to provide support for those who want to innovate. Even those taking on tough challenges still feel secure in their jobs.

STEP 2: Define costovation boundaries and specific strategic initiatives.

Identify your broader innovation goals and boundaries:

❏ Come to consensus on *why* you are innovating. Ensure that your vision for costovation aligns with your organization's overall strategic goals, appetite for change, and innovation portfolio.

❏ Be clear about how far you are willing to go with innovation. Are you looking to disrupt a product line? A business model? A customer? Are you focusing on the core business or on growth areas, or both? This means being explicit about what is out of bounds for this project (e.g., ideas under a certain projected financial size or time to break even).

❏ Define the broad metrics that you will use to define your success.

Summarize your strategic objectives for this particular innovation initiative:

❏ Make sure that you can succinctly state the overarching strategic goal for this innovation project. This should include details on why you are innovating, what it means to win, and where your innovation boundaries are.

❑ Note your organization's competitive advantages—not to box you into traditional lines of thinking, but to act as a starting point for ideation.

Assemble a great team:

❑ Select team members for their ability to generate fresh thinking, to find information quickly, and to tell great stories.

❑ Seek diversity in your team whenever possible—particularly in years of experience in the industry, in thinking style, and in areas of functional expertise.

❑ Set aside protected time for costovation activities.

Are you ready for the next step?

❑ We have developed a clear statement for why we are innovating.

❑ We have defined boundaries for what will be considered, both in the core business and in growth areas, as well as in different functional areas.

❑ We have identified and communicated the criteria by which innovation projects will be judged.

❑ We have selected a team with a wide variety of skills and experiences.

STEP 3: Break out of traditional lines of thinking and choose a costovation focal area.

Identify your industry's assumptions, and practice subverting them:

❑ As individuals or in a group, spend some time exploring what "traditional" thinking means to your organization and industry.

❑ Examine your industry from afar, as if you're wearing binoculars. What would an industry stranger find surprising or baffling?

❏ Take a microscope to your industry, organization, and offerings, and question features individually.

❏ Look through your customers' eyes, instead of your own. How does the way they see the world differ from the way you see them? If at all possible, get out of the conference room and talk to real customers, observe them in real situations, and understand what aspects of products, services, sales, and other cost-drivers really deliver value.

❏ Reconsider the way you classify your customer segments. If you couldn't categorize them around demographics or product lines, how would you do so? How could you organize them around the jobs they are trying to get done?

❏ Rethink the way you view suppliers and other parties in your value chain. What is the usual relationship like? How could you push past "vendor" relationships into something more strategic?

Select a focal point to guide your ideation:

❏ Rally around a single area where you want to excel. Common focal areas in costovation include customer segments, jobs to be done, areas of the business (e.g., marketing, supply chain), and attributes (e.g., convenience, speed). Use your strategic objectives as a guide when choosing your focal area.

Come to a deep understanding of your chosen focal point:

❏ Sift through your existing consumer research and customer knowledge to compile information related to your chosen area of focus. This may mean interviewing other employees not on the costovation team who may have expertise to share.

❏ Take stock of questions about your customers that remain unanswered. Then create a plan for answering them and get started. This may mean conducting customer research (e.g., in-depth interviews, focus groups, in-home ethnographies), as well as bringing in experts or outsiders to weigh in with their opinions.

❑ Bring your target customers to life. Give them a name, describe what they do, and think through their current approaches and the challenges that they face. What motivates them? What frustrates them? What are the jobs that they are trying to get done in their lives, and what is the value to them of getting those jobs done?

Are you ready for the next step?

❑ We have identified our industry assumptions—and questioned each of them.

❑ We have selected a focal point for our costovation efforts to rally around and are committed to using it as an arbiter for choosing what trade-offs to make.

❑ We have come to a deep understanding of that focal area and the customer we aim to serve.

STEP 4: Costovation ideation.

Brainstorm as many ideas as you can:

❑ Go for quantity over quality. We like to start with individual brainstorming, where all ideas are written down on your own, silently, no matter how seemingly foolish or simple. Then share your ideas in a small group and elaborate on them, combining them with others.

❑ After a bit of time away from your list, identify your favorite ideas—keeping in mind that oftentimes multiple ideas can be combined to make a sum greater than its components. Ideally, look for platforms that can support multiple related ideas. Remember to push for innovations throughout the business, not just in your product (e.g., innovate in how the product is made, delivered, or sold).

❑ Develop some criteria for assessing ideas. These can come after you create your ideas, because you may not know what you're looking for until after you've found it.

Assess the ideas:

❑ Score the ideas on a range of metrics, particularly those set forth in your strategic objective. This could include feasibility, risk, investment required, time to return, financial projections, and key customer jobs to be done that are satisfied.

❑ Prioritize a few ideas to move forward.

Are you ready for the next step?

❑ We have brainstormed far and wide, taking care not to nip unconventional ideas too soon.

❑ We have thought of ideas that innovate on areas of the business that customers *do not* see (e.g., how the offering is made, delivered, and sold), as well as on areas that they *do* see.

❑ We have a framework for ideation and prioritizing ideas that doesn't simply favor the easy answers.

❑ We are able to deliver a sixty-second elevator pitch for each idea that we have been working on.

STEP 5: Build out promising ideas, testing early and often.

Develop more detailed plans for prioritized ideas:

❑ Begin to build the business case for each prioritized idea. Provide more details on what it looks like, how it might work, what your organization would need to do to launch it, and what the payoff might be. Research potential competitors and pull any data points you can find.

❑ Determine how early-stage concepts could be integrated into the business. Ensure that your action plans account for changes in trends, regulations, or other macro events.

Experiment, test, and get out in the field to research:

❑ Test your early-stage ideas early and often. This might involve short online concept test surveys or building a prototype to put into a tester's hands. See the break-out box at the end of this checklist for more ideas on how to test cheaply.

❑ List out the top three to five risks and assumptions behind each idea. Pay special attention to validate them.

Create a handoff plan:

❑ Identify who the project will get handed off to as it proceeds toward commercialization and implementation.

❑ Determine what that person will require in terms of support and authority.

❑ Describe clear next steps, which may include more extensive testing (e.g., partial or full pilots).

❑ Articulate possible competitor responses and prepare a comeback for each.

Are you ready for the next step?

❑ We have a strong understanding of the research tools that can help us quickly assess market demand.

❑ We know what questions management will want to have answered before making a decision to invest in a project.

❑ We have clear handoff procedures to ensure that products don't get neglected and killed off as they move into the implementation or commercialization stages.

❑ We embrace fast and inexpensive experimentation, and our compensation and incentive plans reflect the same values.

➤

Low-Cost Ways to Test an Idea

COMPANIES HAVE NO SHORTAGE of ideas. The hard part is identifying which ones to throw resources behind—and when to let an idea go.

We are big fans of testing generously and often. We are surprised at how little testing actually occurs in many businesses before a project becomes massive and full-scale market research is commissioned. But testing doesn't have to be costly or time consuming, especially not at this early stage. Test early and often. Double-check your assumptions. Like with writing, the gold is in iteration and editing.

Here are several techniques that we use in our consulting work to quickly assess the validity of a new idea:

Perform Desk Research. This is often the first stop we make. It sounds overly simple, but don't underestimate what you can learn from the Internet. McDonald's shrimp salad was killed not by a concept test, but by an afternoon of free Internet research on the global supply of shrimp.[1] And one of our recent clients' ideas to create a product specifically for unions was put into new perspective when we performed a quick search into the declining trend in union membership.

Conduct "What Would You Have to Believe" Analysis. This thought exercise is a quick reality check. Start with your end goal, like a revenue target, and walk backwards to determine how many units you would need to sell or the number of long-term customer relationships you would need to cultivate.

In one of our engagements, we were assessing the opportunity to provide business services to large hospitals in Mexico. It was an untapped market that fit nicely with the company's existing services. But our back-of-the-envelope calculations quickly stopped us short: to build a $10 million business, the service would have had to be sold to every single large hospital in the country, at price ranges that were sure to be above the hospitals' appetites.

Perform a Feasibility Assessment. List out all the capabilities you will need to launch this new idea. Want to sell directly to the consumer rather than through the traditional corporate sales channel? You'll need social-media–based marketing skills, a rush of new content, a website that can handle a large volume of transactions, and a team of trained customer-service representatives. Then go through the list, marking the capabilities you have, the ones you can acquire, and the ones you'll have to build from scratch. Compare this table against your strategic objectives and ensure that the proposed project is within scope.

Send Out a Quick Survey. Market-research surveys don't have to be huge undertakings with thousands of respondents. You can often get great quick feedback using cheap online surveys or five-minute live "intercept" surveys. While assessing wellness concepts for a health system, for instance, we intercepted people outside a health-food store. It was a purposely skewed sample population. The people who shopped at a health-food store, we figured, would be most interested in the new wellness concept. If we couldn't get positive interest from that crowd, it could be pointless to push further.

Exploit Similar Situations. A client of ours was exploring a new way to distribute its products in emerging market megacities, like São Paolo or Delhi. It would have been costly to fly a team out to Delhi, so we encouraged the company to start with a megacity closer to home, like New York City. The idea was to work out the kinks and test broad assumptions before further investment was made.

Concept Test. The key to concept testing is to make the interview situation as real as possible. That means using prototypes, images, and visits to the place where the product would be consumed. In the late 1990s, Stephen was testing flat-screen televisions in the classic fishbowl focus group—the kind in drab office buildings with one-way glass. The response was pitiful. The respondents didn't care about having a slimmer TV. They didn't know why we were so excited that you could hang it on a wall. Customers aren't great at knowing what they want, and our mistake was to ask for their opinions in a situation that was totally unrealistic and as far as possible from the comfort and coziness of their living rooms. It led to an inaccurate response.

Get Scrappy. There are countless inexpensive and quick ways to test ideas. You could gauge demand for a new offering by monitoring clicks on a Google AdWords campaign that leads to a test website. You could speak for thirty minutes with an expert in the field. You can interrogate people by slipping behind them in the long Starbucks line at an industry convention (yes, we've done that). Hey, Charlie, a digital health app that helps opiate addicts prevent relapses, first validated its idea through a poll and discussion thread that it started on a drug-recovery thread on Reddit. BloomThat, a flower delivery startup that promises flowers in ninety minutes, tested its concept on a Valentine's Day by buying flowers in bulk from the San Francisco Flower Mart, assembling them into bouquets, wrapping them with butcher paper, and putting out Facebook ads promising delivery in ninety minutes. They didn't make a huge profit, but revenue wasn't the point of the test. The most important thing was that they confirmed customer interest in their idea.

/ acknowledgments /

This book was six years in the making, and credit goes to many people for making it happen. We were first introduced to the idea of costovation by Graeme Armstrong, who led R&D and innovation for the Dutch chemicals and coatings giant Akzo Nobel. His quest to see what innovation tools could do for costs led us in unanticipated and intriguing directions. We were also influenced by coaching from other clients along the way, especially Brian Newman, Executive Vice President for Global Operations at PepsiCo.

I worked for six years with Harvard Business School Professor Clayton Christensen, and his thinking—along with the constant stimulation of my outstanding partners at Christensen's consulting firm Innosight—shaped my outlook in many ways. In particular, Clay originated the concept of "jobs to be done" which is foundational to finding costovation opportunities.

My colleagues at New Markets Advisors, both current and past, were essential to this journey as well. Particular thanks go to Greg Ainsworth, Dave Farber, Kara Robinson, and Tess Vorselen. And, of course, Jennifer Luo Law was absolutely core to making this book happen. Kudos go to our editor at HarperCollins Leadership, Timothy Burgard, and our agent at Trident, Don Fehr.

Writing books is not a family-friendly endeavor. The work creeps into nights and weekends meant for other duties. So special thanks for support go to my wife, Jessica, and our three boys Wyatt, Cyrus, and Monty. Jessica also read over several drafts and made innumerable helpful suggestions.

Finally, thanks go to all the audiences I've tried this material out on as it was still being developed. They've helped sharpen our thinking, and I certainly hope they continue to do so.

—*Stephen Wunker*

As a first-time author, I underestimated just how much intellectual, technical, and moral support goes into writing a book. Now that I've emerged on the other side, I owe great thanks to the many people who cheered me on and gave this project wings.

My colleagues at New Markets, both past and present, were foundational in shaping and challenging the ideas in this book. David Farber in particular was a wonderful sounding board, and his encyclopedic knowledge of case studies meant I never lacked inspiration. Jessica Wattman was invaluable in helping me find my writing voice. And of course, I am deeply grateful to my co-author Stephen Wunker, whose intellect and wit give me so much to aspire to. He has selflessly mentored me over many years, and it has been a privilege writing this book together.

I am always thankful to my parents, Hongfei Lin and John Law, who taught me grit and optimism by example. My brother Canyon Law is my go-to for comedic therapy, and Andy O'Hara and Kurt MacDonald originally inspired my interest in writing way back in high school. And to my best friend and soulmate, Collin De La Bruere, I owe special thanks. He listened to many rambling book thoughts, offered boundless suggestions, and pretended to be busy on his laptop next to me so that I wouldn't feel bad about spending yet another evening writing. This project has been part of our lives for years, and its success is as much part of my life as it is his.

—*Jennifer Luo Law*

/ notes /

CHAPTER ONE

1. Planet Fitness 2016 Annual Report
2. "J.D. Power 2017 Health and Fitness Center Satisfaction Report," *J.D. Power,* 2017
3. "Financial & Operations Research," International Health, Racquet & Sportsclub Association
4. Leslie Patton, "McDonald's seen overhauling US menu from 145 choices," *Bloomberg,* 17 May 2013
5. Susan Berfield, "Why the McWrap is so important to McDonald's," *Bloomberg,* 3 July 2013
6. Julie Jargon, "McDonald's says its restaurants got too complicated," *Wall Street Journal,* 23 January 2014
7. Whitney Filloon, "Is McDonald's All-Day Breakfast Turning Out to be a Big McFailure?" *Eater,* 16 October 2015
8. "Deloitte's fourth biennial cost survey: cost-improvement practices and trends in the Fortune 1000," *Deloitte,* April 2016
9. "Real average hourly earnings increased 0.6 percent over the year ended May 2017," Bureau of Labor Statistics, 19 June 2017

CHAPTER TWO

1. Zimride, meanwhile, continued to be profitable and was sold to Enterprise Holdings in 2013.
2. Sarah Max, "Catering to Boomers, a Cell Phone Company Takes Off," *Entrepreneur,* 30 July 2013

CHAPTER THREE

1. Earl Sasser, "Benihana of Tokyo," *Harvard Business School,* November 1972

CHAPTER FOUR

1. Michael Porter, "What is Strategy?," *Harvard Business Review,* November-December 1996
2. Rob Wengel, "How to Flip 85% Misses to 85% Hits: Lessons From the Nielsen Breakthrough Innovation Project," *Neilsen,* 24 June 2014
3. "Inside Starbucks' ambitious plan to combat the 'seismic shift' that could kill its business," *South China Morning Post,* 8 December 2016
4. "Starbucks Q1 2017 Results," *Starbucks*
5. Terrence O'Keefe, "Suppliers are key partners in innovation team at Trader Joe's: Interview with Doug Rauch, former president at Trader Joe's," *WATTAgNet.com,* 30 October 2014
6. Serena Ng, "Soap Opera: Amazon Moves In With P&G," *Wall Street Journal,* 14 October 2013
7. Soizic Briand, "Voici le classement des enseignes préférées des Français," *Challenges,* 24 September 2014
8. Gayle Martin and Obert Pimhidzai, "Education and Health Services in Kenya," *World Bank,* July 2013
9. James Macharia, "Kenyan MPs defy president, hike pay to 130 times minimum wage," *Reuters,* 28 May 2013

CHAPTER FIVE

1. "Chile," World Bank Data
2. Thomson One Banker database, June 2011; M Scilly, "The Average Merchandise Turnover for Clothing Stores," *Chron*
3. John Markoff, "No Sailors Needed: Robot Sailboats Scour the Oceans for Data," *The New York Times,* 4 September 2016
4. Janelle Nanos, "MIT researchers develop a shape-shifting pasta," *Boston Globe,* 5 June 2017
5. Elizabeth Glagowski, "Build-A-Bear Builds a Brand Around Customer Experience," *Customer Strategist,* September 2013
6. Simone Hill, "Evolution of the KitchenAid Mixer," The Knot
7. Linda Tischler, "The 'Product of the Year' Awards: The Grammy's of the Walgreens Scene," *Fast Company,* 3 February 2010
8. Arvind Verma, "Case Study: Smart Cars," Symbiosis Institute of Management Studies
9. Michael Horn, "The Rise of AltSchool and Other Micro-Schools," *Education Next,* Summer 2015

10. Lam Thuy Vo, "How Much Does the Government Spend to Send a Kid to Public School?" *NPR*, 21 June 2012

11. "Global Connected Commerce: Is E-tail Therapy the New Retail Therapy?" *Nielsen*, January 2016

12. Statista, Number of Skiers and Snowboarders in the USA; Megan Barber, "Ski Industry Expert Says 31% of Today's Ski Areas Are Dying," *Curbed Ski*, 29 January 2015

13. Mike Gorrell, "With Epic Pass sales booming, Vail plans to add more fine dining, family fun to Park City Mountain Resort," *The Salt Lake Tribune*, 11 December 2017

14. "Number of specialty coffee shops in the United States from 1991 to 2015," Statista, 2017; Park Jae-hyuk, "Korea is 'republic of coffee'," *Korea Times*, April 2017

15. "Korea Coffee Market Brief Update," USDA Foreign Agricultural Service, 31 December 2015

16. Steven Kurtz, "Is This Store the Best-Kept Secret in Fashion?" *The New York Times*, 15 March 2007

17. "ColaLife Operational Trial Zambia: Endline Survey Report," United Kingdom Department for International Development, June 2014

18. Demetri Sevastopulo, "Li & Fung's Strategy to Make the Maths Work," *Financial Times*, 2 June 2014

CHAPTER SIX

1. "What to Do When There Are Too Many Product Choices on the Store Shelves?" *Consumer Reports*, January 2014

2. Alina Selyukh, "Discount Grocers Aldi and Lidl Give U.S. Stores a Run for Their Money," *NPR*, 27 September 2017

3. Neal Raisman, "The Cost of College Attrition at Four-Year Colleges & Universities," *Educational Policy Institute*, February 2013

4. Steven Cohen, "Differentials in the Concentration of Health Expenditures Across Population Subgroups in the U.S., 2012," *Agency for Healthcare Research and Quality*, September 2014

5. "About Us," *Cameron Hughes Wine*

6. Laura Burgess, "Why Some Wines Are So Damn Expensive— Breaking Down the Cost of a Bottle of Wine," *Vinepair*, 12 June 2015

7. Jeffrey Mitchell, "FastStats 2016: The Rising Cost of Independent School Tuition," SAIS, 17 February 2016; Jordan Yadoo, "Private

School Is Becoming Out of Reach for Middle-Class Americans," *Bloomberg*, 19 July 2017

8. Ted Cooper, "Everyone Is Getting Rich in the Coffee Business," *The Motley Fool*, 15 January 2014

9. Fitz Tepper, "Framebridge adds $17M in funding as it takes custom framing mainstream," *Techcrunch*, 13 July 2017

CHAPTER SEVEN

1. Nathan Eagle, "Getting the next billion online lies in affordability, not accessibility," *The Next Web*, 25 February 2016

2. David Cutler, "Why Does Health Care Cost So Much in America? Ask Harvard's David Cutler," *PBS News Hour*, 19 November 2013

3. Scott Horsley, "Despite an Economy on the Rise, American Paychecks Remain Stuck," *NPR*, 26 May 2015

4. Lawrence Mishel, Elise Gould, and Josh Bivens, "Wage Stagnation in Nine Charts," *Economic Policy Institute*, 6 January 2015

CHECKLIST FOR GETTING STARTED

1. Janet Adamy, "For McDonald's, It's a Wrap," *Wall Street Journal*, 30 January 2007

/ index /